The E.R.T. Framework™

How to Build Empathy, *Strengthen Resilience, and* Create Lasting Transformation

Dwayne Buckingham, PhD, LCSW-C, BCD, PCC

The E.R.T. Doctor™ — Empathy & Resilience

www.buckinghamcgroup.com

For permissions, licensing, training, or speaking inquiries, contact:
info@buckinghamcgroup.com or visit us at www.ertinstitute.org

Printed in the United States of America

Editing, book cover design and interior formatting by Buckingham Press

ISBN: 979-8-9953272-0-2

Library of Congress Control Number: Available Upon Request

First Edition: 2026

Dedication

This book is dedicated to every individual who has ever felt unseen, unheard, or underestimated.

To the soldiers who carried invisible wounds, the families who fought to stay together, the leaders who carried burdens in silence, and the communities who refused to let hardship define them—you are the reason this work exists.

To my family, who taught me resilience by example and showed me the power of empathy in action—your love has been my anchor.

And to every person who believes that transformation is possible: this book is for you.

Acknowledgments

No journey is ever walked alone, and this book is no exception.

First, I thank God for the vision, strength, and perseverance to complete this work. Without His guidance, none of this would be possible.

To my family—thank you for your unwavering love, encouragement, and patience. You have been my safe space, my strength, and my greatest reminder of why empathy and resilience matter.

To my military brothers and sisters: serving alongside you shaped my understanding of sacrifice, resilience, and leadership. The lessons learned in uniform echo throughout these pages.

To the countless clients, leaders, students, and community members I've had the privilege of serving—you are the heartbeat of this approach. Your stories, struggles, and triumphs breathed life into these pages.

To my colleagues at Buckingham Consulting Group and partners across the globe—thank you for believing in this vision and for helping me carry it forward.

And finally, to every reader: thank you for opening your mind and heart to this journey. My hope is that you don't just read these words, but that you live them—and in doing so, spark transformation in your own life and in the lives of others.

Preface

The world is full of noise—opinions, strategies, quick fixes, and commentary that sound useful but rarely speak to what people truly carry. Despite having more information than ever, people continue to feel emotionally exhausted, relationally disconnected, and spiritually depleted. Leaders are burning out. Families are under pressure. Communities struggle to stay together while the systems meant to support them often fail.

I did not write this book to add noise. I wrote it after more than twenty-five years of seeing people seek relief, direction, and healing, only to find that information alone does not transform. In counseling rooms, military settings, executive spaces, classrooms, and community conversations, I saw one truth: people need to be understood, need strength to endure, and need a pathway to help pain produce more than survival.

This shaped the E.R.T. Framework—Empathy, Resilience, and Transformation. Empathy helps people feel seen without shame. Resilience helps them stand when life presses hard. Transformation: not a surface adjustment, but a reorganization of how a person lives, leads, relates, and recovers. This book exists because change alone is not enough when people need renewal from the inside out.

So why this book? Because shallow solutions are no longer enough. Individuals, families, professionals, leaders, and communities need a framework that is both human and practical. Empathy, resilience, and transformation are not abstract; they are disciplines that change what comes next.

Table of Contents

INTRODUCTION

Why Empathy, Resilience, and Transformation Matter Now

We are living in a time of extraordinary access and fracture. People can communicate instantly, yet struggle to feel genuinely known. Organizations generate data faster than ever, but still fail to understand the human cost of their decisions. Communities can mobilize around urgent causes but still exhaust themselves. Outrage is not endurance.

Too many people know how to react, but not how to recover. Too many systems manage performance, but do not cultivate wholeness. Too many leaders move fast, but do not move people well. These are reasons why the E.R.T. Framework™ matters.

Without empathy, people do not feel safe to tell the truth. Without resilience, insight collapses under real-life pressure. Without transformation, awareness becomes sophisticated stagnation—many words, little change. The modern world does not only suffer from a lack of information. It suffers from poor integration.

I am Dr. Dwayne L. Buckingham, known as The E.R. Doctor™. I developed the E.R.T. Framework™ over more than 25 years in the mental health industry and through service to over 40,000 individuals, couples, and families worldwide. I have worked in counseling rooms, military settings, leadership environments, and community spaces where the stakes were real and the pain was not theoretical. Across those spaces, I saw again and again that people do not simply need advice. They need disciplined understanding, adaptive strength, and a pathway toward meaningful change.

Empathy is the first pillar. Real growth rarely begins where people feel judged, dismissed, or emotionally unsafe. Resilience is the second pillar. The truth, once faced, must still be lived through. Transformation is the third pillar. The goal is not simply to cope better for a moment, but to become more grounded, more congruent, and more capable of living with integrity over time. These three pillars belong together. Empathy without resilience can overwhelm. Resilience without empathy can harden. Transformation without both often becomes performance rather than substance.

In the chapters ahead, you will move through the foundations of the framework. You will learn the practical structure that supports it, as well as the values and beliefs that anchor it. We will look at the domains in which it can be applied and the research that supports why this approach is both humane and sound. My goal is not merely to inspire you. It is to equip you—to help you understand the framework, examine your own life through it, and apply it personally, relationally, professionally, and collectively.

PART I

The Foundation

CHAPTER 1

Why Empathy, Resilience, and Transformation Matter in Today's World

We live in an age of speed, stimulation, and strain. People can reach each other instantly, yet still miss one another emotionally. Leaders drive outcomes, but often neglect the human cost. Systems grow more efficient, but less trustworthy. Communities grow louder, but not more connected. Individuals collect information, credentials, and responsibilities, yet quietly fall apart inside. That is the modern problem. Activity surrounds us, but we are not always anchored in what helps humans grow well.

Burnout is everywhere. Disconnection is common. Fragile systems are exposed the moment pressure rises. Leadership often becomes reactive rather than reflective. And many of the changes people pursue—personally, professionally, or collectively—remain shallow because they address performance without addressing people. We know more than ever, yet many people still do not know how to remain grounded, connected, and transformed under pressure. That is why this book begins here. The world does not simply need more compassion in isolation, nor more toughness in isolation. It needs a more integrated human response. It needs empathy, resilience, and transformation to work together.

Empathy matters because people rarely heal, grow, or lead well in environments where they feel unseen. Resilience matters because understanding alone cannot carry a person through adversity. Transformation matters because the goal is not merely to endure another difficult season, but to become wiser, steadier, and more aligned because of what has been faced. The crises of our time are not solved by urgency alone. They require a framework that helps people connect honestly, adapt effectively, and change sustainably.

I have sat with executives who felt crushed by the weight of expectations but could not admit it because they were supposed to have it all together. I have counseled soldiers returning from war who struggled to speak about their pain because they did not want to burden their families. I have listened to single mothers carrying entire households on their shoulders who said, in one form or another, "I just need someone to hear me without judging me." What they all had in common was not occupation, background, or status. What they shared was the longing to be understood and the need for a strength deeper than performance. That is where the E.R.T. Framework™ begins.

The Problem Beneath the Pressure

People often fail not because they lack information, but because information alone does not create wisdom, trust, or capacity. A person can know what to do and still not do it well if they are emotionally disconnected, overwhelmed, or inwardly depleted. A leader can attend every training, master every strategy, and still damage a team if they lead without empathy. A family can understand what healthy communication should look like and still remain trapped in defensive patterns if nobody has the resilience to stay engaged when emotions rise. A community can call for change and still reproduce the same dysfunction if its efforts are reactive, fractured, or shallow.

This is why so many people struggle in three predictable ways. First, they try to live on information without empathy. They become knowledgeable but disconnected. They know facts, strategies, and talking points, but they do not know how to sit with pain, understand context, or build trust. Second, they try to survive pressure without resilience. They push, suppress, perform, and endure until exhaustion masquerades as strength. Third, they pursue change without transformation. They temporarily adjust behavior, adopt new language, or react to a crisis, but the deeper patterns beneath the surface remain untouched.

That is why the E.R.T. Framework™ matters now. It addresses not just what people know, but how they connect, how they recover, and how they change. It offers a model of human development that is just as relevant to leaders as to families, clinicians, educators, coaches, communities, and institutions. It is not designed merely to help people cope with the moment. It is designed to help people become more grounded, more adaptive, and more transformative in the way they live and lead.

To understand how lasting human growth actually happens, it helps to see the E.R.T. Framework™ as a connected model: empathy as the foundation, resilience as the engine, and transformation as the outcome.

This visual is more than a diagram. It is the book's architecture and the framework's logic. Each pillar matters on its own, but their true power emerges in how they work together.

Empathy as the Foundation

Empathy is the foundation because human beings do not flourish where they feel unseen. At its core, empathy is about recognizing another person's emotional reality and taking their experience seriously enough to engage with care. It is the ability to say, "Your inner world matters, and I am willing to understand it before I rush to correct it." That kind of presence changes people. It lowers defensiveness. It builds trust. It opens the possibility of truth without immediate shame.

Empathy is not weakness. It is not an agreement. It is not the abandonment of standards, boundaries, or discernment. It is a disciplined form of human recognition. It allows people to feel heard without being indulged and understood without being reduced. In leadership, empathy helps people feel valued rather than merely managed. In counseling and coaching, it creates the relational safety needed for honesty. In families and communities, it reminds people that connection is not a luxury. It is part of what makes repair and growth possible.

Without empathy, people may still comply, perform, or survive, but they often do so in emotionally disconnected ways. Systems may look functional while trust erodes beneath the surface. Relationships may continue while intimacy weakens. Teams may produce while morale quietly collapses. Empathy is foundational because it restores the human element that performance alone can never replace.

Resilience as the Engine

If empathy is what opens the heart, resilience is what carries the weight. Resilience is the engine because it gives people the capacity to endure adversity, recover from setbacks, adapt under pressure, and keep moving without losing themselves in the process. It is not stoicism. It is not denial. It is not an emotional shutdown disguised as strength. Real resilience does not ignore pain. It learns how to move through pain without being mastered by it.

We live in a world of uncertainty. Jobs shift. Economies fluctuate. Families experience loss. Institutions face crises. Communities absorb injustice. In that kind of world, resilience is not a luxury. It is a necessity. But it must be understood correctly. A resilient person is not someone who never feels overwhelmed. A resilient person is someone who learns to recover, adjust, and remain grounded when life puts pressure on them.

This is why empathy alone is not enough. A person can care deeply and still burn out. A leader can understand everyone around them and still crumble under the weight of constant demand. A helper can absorb other people's pain and lose the strength needed to remain effective. Without resilience, empathy can become exhaustion. Resilience keeps empathy from collapsing under the burden of reality. It gives endurance to compassion and steadiness to care.

Transformation as the Outcome

Transformation is the outcome because the goal of this framework is not simply to feel more or endure more. The goal is to change in ways that last. Transformation is what happens when empathy and resilience work together long enough and deeply enough to alter how a person lives, leads, relates, and responds. It is more than a temporary change. It is more than inspiration. It is a deeper reorganization of the self.

Many people experience change without transformation. They make a short-term adjustment, adopt a new habit, or respond to a crisis, but once pressure lifts, they return to familiar patterns. Transformation is different. Transformation becomes visible in how people handle conflict, recover from setbacks, relate to others, carry responsibility, and stay aligned with truth under stress. It shows up not only in what people say, but in how they live.

That is why transformation belongs at the top of the framework. It is the outcome of connection plus capacity. When people are understood well and strengthened wisely, they are better positioned to become different in durable ways. Transformation is not magic. It is what becomes possible when empathy creates connection and resilience builds strength. In that sense, transformation is not the beginning of the process. It is the fruit of a well-executed process.

Why This Framework Matters Now

The old ways of leading, serving, and surviving are breaking down. Information overload, emotional fatigue, a shallow performance culture, and systemic strain are forcing people to ask a deeper question: what kind of human beings do we need to become to live and lead well in this world? The answer cannot be reduced to skill alone. It must include how we understand others, how we endure hardship, and how we change in response to what we face.

That is why the E.R.T. Framework™ is not just a theory placed on a whiteboard. It is a way of understanding what helps people, teams, families, and communities move from disconnection to depth, from fragility to strength, and from reaction to transformation. It is a model I have practiced as a psychotherapist, military officer, coach, and consultant. It is a framework I have seen help heal families, strengthen leaders, deepen organizations, and restore hope to people who believed they had nothing left to give.

And now, through this book, I want to place a framework in your hands. Because no matter your role—parent, student, professional, educator, leader, advocate, or caregiver—you will face moments when empathy and resilience will determine whether pressure produces collapse or transformation.

This book is your invitation to choose something deeper than survival.

Reflection Questions

1. Where do I see burnout, disconnection, fragile systems, reactive leadership, or shallow change most clearly in the world around me?
2. When have I experienced information without empathy, pressure without resilience, or change without transformation?
3. Which of the three pillars—empathy, resilience, or transformation—feels strongest in my life right now, and which needs the most development?

Action Step

Identify one current situation in your life where the E.R.T. Framework™ can be applied. Ask yourself what empathy would require, what resilience would demand, and what transformation might make possible.

Affirmation

"I can choose connection without losing strength, and I can build strength without losing my humanity."

The rest of this book carefully builds on that sequence. We begin with empathy because connection creates the conditions in which truth can be told, defenses can soften, and change can begin. Before resilience can sustain the journey and transformation can become the outcome, we must first understand what empathy really is.

CHAPTER 2

The Human Blueprint

Understanding Empathy

Empathy is often treated like a soft skill, a personality trait, or a moral preference. It is more than that. In the E.R.T. Framework™, empathy is a foundational human capacity. It is part of what makes honest connection, meaningful healing, and lasting transformation possible. Before people can change deeply, they often need to feel seen accurately. Before they can trust the process of growth, they often need to know they are not being reduced to a problem, a diagnosis, a role, or a failure. Empathy creates that first opening.

That is why empathy comes first in this framework. It is the blueprint because it reminds us that human beings are wired not only for survival, but for connection. We are shaped by whether we are heard or dismissed, understood or misread, welcomed or merely managed. A person can have resources, structure, and even opportunity, but still feel emotionally stranded if no one is willing to engage their humanity with care and accuracy. Empathy closes that gap. It does not fix everything, but it changes the environment in which healing and growth become possible.

In a world filled with hurry, division, overload, and performance, empathy becomes both harder and more necessary. People are often surrounded by noise yet starved for understanding. Leaders are pressured to produce. Families are stretched thin. Communities are carrying pain that is often politicized, minimized, or ignored. In that kind of world, empathy is not weakness. It is a disciplined human presence. It is the ability to recognize what another person may be carrying without rushing to control, correct, or dismiss them. And in this framework, that kind of presence is where the work begins.

What Empathy Is

Let me make something clear from the start: empathy is not sympathy. Sympathy looks from a distance and says, "I feel sorry for you." Empathy steps into the space beside someone and says, "I want to understand what this feels like for you." Sympathy can pity. Empathy chooses presence. Sympathy often preserves distance. Empathy narrows it.

In the E.R.T. Framework™, empathy is a grounded form of human understanding. It is the capacity to recognize another person's emotional reality, take their experience seriously, and engage them in a way that lowers defensiveness and increases trust. It is not pity, permissiveness, or emotional fusion. It is not an agreement with everything someone says or does. It is not the abandonment of truth, boundaries, or discernment. Empathy simply means we refuse to treat people as if their inner world does not matter.

When people are in pain, they often do not need immediate correction nearly as much as they need accurate human contact. Think about the last time you went through something difficult. Most people in that moment do not want a cliché. They do not want a speech. They do not want to be rushed past their pain. They want someone who can sit with them honestly enough to say, "I may not know everything you feel, but I am willing to understand what this is like for you." That is empathy.

I have seen the power of that in practice. Several years ago, I counseled a young man who had returned from deployment overseas. He carried memories that haunted him at night and made him restless during the day. He was guarded, tense, and convinced that no one would understand what he had been through. He told me, "Doc, no one's going to understand what I've seen." I could have rushed into explanation, labels, or technique. Instead, I leaned into empathy. I told him, "You're right. I may never fully understand what you've seen. But I want to understand how it feels to carry it. If you're willing, I'll walk through it with you." That moment shifted the room. His shoulders relaxed. His tone softened. And slowly, he began to open. What made the difference was not my title. It was empathy that made truth feel survivable.

Types and Dimensions of Empathy

One reason empathy is so often misunderstood is that people talk about it as if it were one simple instinct. It is not. In this framework, empathy includes more than one dimension, and those dimensions matter.

The first is emotional attunement. Emotional attunement is the capacity to register and respond to another person's felt experience. It is what allows you to notice grief in someone's silence, fear in their defensiveness, or exhaustion behind their irritability. Emotional attunement helps people feel less alone by communicating that their inner reality is not invisible.

The second is disciplined understanding. This is the decision to slow down, suspend distortion, and listen carefully enough to understand what another person may be carrying without rushing to fix, challenge, or dismiss them. Disciplined understanding matters because emotional awareness alone can be imprecise. A person may feel another's pain without understanding its context. This is why empathy must include thoughtfulness, patience, and restraint. It is not enough to react emotionally. We must also learn to understand responsibly.

The third is a compassionate response. Compassionate response is the willingness to let understanding shape humane action. Sometimes that action looks like presence. Sometimes it looks like support. Sometimes it looks like advocacy. Sometimes it looks like truth delivered with dignity. Compassionate response keeps empathy from becoming passive observation. It reminds us that to understand another person well, we should change how we engage them.

These distinctions matter. Emotional attunement without discipline can become over-identification. A person may feel so strongly with someone else that they lose clarity. Disciplined understanding without attunement can become detached observation. A person may analyze another human being without ever truly connecting. Compassion without either can become performative. In the E.R.T. Framework™, healthy empathy requires all three dimensions working together. That is what makes empathy more than sentiment. It becomes a grounded, relational capacity that builds trust and enables honest engagement.

There is science behind this. Empathy is not merely a nice idea. Research in psychology and neuroscience supports the idea that human beings are wired for emotional resonance and social understanding. Our brains and bodies are responsive to others' experiences. That is one reason we cringe when someone else falls, tear up during a powerful story, or feel moved when another person succeeds against the odds. But empathy is not entirely automatic. Bias, fear, overload, hurry, and self-protection can mute it. That is why empathy must be treated not only as a capacity, but as a practice. It can be strengthened, neglected, distorted, or refined.

When Empathy Is Misunderstood or Misused

Empathy is often either overpraised or unfairly attacked. Some people treat it as though it is the answer to every human problem. Others describe it as weak, manipulative, biased, or morally dangerous. Both extremes misunderstand it. Empathy is not a god, nor is it a threat. It is a human capacity that can be practiced wisely or distorted poorly.

Part of the confusion stems from how people use the word empathy to mean different things. Sometimes they mean emotional resonance or feeling with another person. Sometimes they mean perspective-taking or understanding another person's internal world. Sometimes they mean compassion, or the willingness to respond humanely.

When those categories are blurred, empathy gets blamed for things that are actually caused by emotional coercion, poor boundaries, manipulation, or undisciplined reasoning.

That concern is not entirely imaginary. People can misuse pain to pressure for agreement. They can imply that if you truly care, you must automatically affirm their beliefs, choices, or conclusions. But that is not healthy empathy. That is emotional pressure disguised as moral sensitivity. Empathy is not agreement. It is not authority. And it should never replace discernment. Someone's pain deserves humane attention, but pain alone does not settle every ethical, relational, or social question.

Empathy can also become narrow if it is not disciplined. Human beings tend to respond more intensely to suffering that feels vivid, familiar, or personal. We often care more quickly about people who resemble us, agree with us, or belong to our group. That means empathy, when left unexamined, can become tribal, uneven, and reactive. But this does not mean empathy itself is defective. It means empathy must be guided by reflection, values, and emotional regulation.

This is where the E.R.T. Framework™ makes an important contribution. E.R.T. does not stop with empathy. Empathy is the first condition, not the final answer. It helps us see clearly, slow our assumptions, and engage people with greater humanity. But empathy without resilience can leave a person emotionally flooded, reactive, or burned out. What many critics call the danger of empathy is often really the danger of empathy without strength.

The healthier path is not less empathy, but better empathy. Mature empathy says, "I can understand your pain without surrendering my convictions, and I can hold my convictions without denying your humanity." That kind of empathy does not weaken truth. It humanizes it. It does not replace principle. It helps principle travel with dignity. And when empathy is joined with resilience, it becomes a foundation for change that is both humane and durable.

Why Empathy Is Not Enough by Itself

Empathy is foundational, but it is not the whole framework. It opens the heart and clears the relational space, but what it makes possible must still be carried, practiced, and sustained. That is where many people struggle. They can feel deeply, understand accurately, and care sincerely, yet still become overwhelmed, depleted, or immobilized when life presses hard. In those moments, empathy alone is not enough.

This is why resilience must follow empathy in the E.R.T. Framework™. Empathy helps a person recognize what is true. Resilience helps a person stay grounded in that truth without collapsing beneath it. Empathy allows us to see pain more clearly. Resilience gives us the capacity to carry what we see, adapt under pressure, recover from setbacks, and continue forward without losing ourselves. Without resilience, empathy can become exhaustion. With resilience, empathy becomes sustainable.

That is why empathy is the first pillar rather than the whole framework. It creates connection, lowers defensiveness, and opens the way for honest engagement. But the work of growth does not end with recognition. It must move into endurance, adaptation, and strength. If empathy helps us understand pain, people, and context more honestly, resilience helps us carry that truth without being swallowed by it.

So, the question is no longer only whether we can feel with others. The deeper question is whether we can remain strong enough to stay present, wise enough to respond well, and grounded enough to keep growing through what we encounter. That is the work of the next pillar. That is the strength within.

Reflection Questions

- When have you experienced the difference between sympathy and empathy in your own life? What made one feel more meaningful than the other?
- Which dimension of empathy comes most naturally to you: emotional attunement, disciplined understanding, or compassionate response? Which one needs more growth?

- In what ways have you seen empathy misunderstood, misused, or confused with agreement?
- What happens in your life or leadership when empathy is present, but resilience is weak?
- How might stronger resilience help you practice empathy without becoming overwhelmed, reactive, or depleted?

CHAPTER 3

The Strength Within

Understanding Resilience

In the E.R.T. Framework™, resilience is not rugged individualism dressed up as strength. It is not emotional suppression, denial, or the false heroism of pretending you are unaffected by what hurts. Resilience is the adaptive capacity to stay engaged with reality, recover with honesty, and keep moving without abandoning your humanity. That is what makes resilience specifically E.R.T.-shaped. It is strengthened by empathy, not separated from it. It allows people to metabolize pain without becoming defined by it, and it prepares the ground for transformation by teaching the mind, body, and spirit how to keep practicing truth under pressure.

When people hear the word resilience, they often picture someone gritting their teeth and pushing through hardship. "Tough it out," we say. "Keep moving." While there is a certain strength in perseverance, true resilience is not about pretending pain doesn't exist or forcing yourself to be invincible. Resilience is not the absence of struggle. It is the ability to face struggle and still find a way to rise. It's about bending without breaking, adapting without losing yourself, and transforming adversity into strength.

The Myth of the "Strong Person"

In many cultures, especially in America, we glorify the idea of the "strong person"—the one who never cries, never asks for help, and always has the right answer. I've seen this myth in corporate leaders who believe they must be bulletproof, in soldiers who think asking for help makes them weak, and in parents who think holding back their tears makes them better role models. But here's the truth: denial is not resilience. Suppression is not strength.

Real resilience allows space for vulnerability. It acknowledges the wound but refuses to let the wound define the story.

Story:

I once worked with a single mother raising three children after her partner walked away. At first, she described herself as "barely surviving." But as I listened, I noticed resilience woven through her story: how she created routines for her kids, how she budgeted every dollar with precision, how she kept showing up despite exhaustion.

I told her: "You may feel like you're barely holding on, but you are demonstrating resilience every single day. Your children will remember not just the struggle, but the strength you showed in the midst of it."

Resilience doesn't always look glamorous. Often, it looks like persistence in the ordinary.

The Role of Empathy in Building Resilience

Here's where the E.R.T. Framework™ is unique: resilience is not built in isolation. Research shows that people who feel supported are more likely to recover from setbacks. That's because empathy is fuel for resilience. When we know someone sees us, believes in us, and walks beside us, we are far more likely to rise again.

Think of a time you were going through something difficult. Did someone's belief in you make it easier to keep going? That was empathy, strengthening your resilience.

Resilience in Crisis

During my time as Chief of Resilience and Psychological Services at Walter Reed National Military Medical Center, I saw resilience tested daily. Soldiers came back from deployments with visible and invisible wounds. Families carried the weight of long separations, grief, and reintegration struggles. In those moments, resilience wasn't about dismissing the pain. It was about helping people find meaning, hope, and a path forward. Some did it through counseling. Others through faith. Others through community support. No matter the method, the common thread was that they didn't face adversity alone.

The Five Skills of Resilience

Resilience is not just a trait you're born with. It's a set of skills you can develop:

1. **Emotional Regulation** – The ability to manage stress and stay grounded under pressure.
2. **Cognitive Flexibility** – The capacity to reframe negative events and see new possibilities.

3. **Problem-Solving** – Taking practical steps even in uncertainty.
4. **Social Connection** – Building networks of support that provide encouragement and perspective.
5. **Purpose** – Anchoring your life in meaning bigger than the moment.

These five skills can be learned, practiced, and strengthened.

Why Resilience Matters in Every Sphere

- **In Families**: Resilience helps children grow into confident adults who can handle setbacks.
- **In Workplaces:** Resilient employees adapt to change, drive innovation, and reduce burnout.
- **In Communities**: Resilience fuels collective healing after trauma or disaster.
- **In Leadership:** Resilient leaders create cultures where challenges become opportunities.

Resilience Without Empathy

Just as empathy without resilience leads to burnout, resilience without empathy leads to isolation. Yes, you can push through challenges on your own. But without empathy, you risk becoming hardened, disconnected, or even cynical. Some people survive but never thrive because they never let others in.

The E.R.T. Framework™ insists that resilience must be paired with empathy. Together, they create transformation that is sustainable and life-giving.

The Transformation Equation

So, here's the formula again: Empathy + Resilience = Transformation.

- Empathy says: "I see you and I am with you."
- Resilience says: "I can rise even when life knocks me down."
- Together, they say: "I will not only survive this—I will be transformed by it."

This is the heart of the E.R.T. Framework™, and it is the heart of this book.

Reflection Questions

1. What is one setback I've overcome that proved my resilience?
2. How do I currently cope with challenges—healthy or unhealthy?

Action Step

Write down three resilience strategies that have helped you in the past and commit to using them in the future.

Affirmation

"I carry the strength to rise within me."

Empathy helps people feel safe enough to face what is real. Resilience helps them remain present long enough for a new way of living to take root. When those two pillars are practiced together, the result is not merely endurance. It is transformation.

CHAPTER 4

Transformation

From Insight to Lasting Change

Why Transformation Deserves Its Own Chapter

Too many people talk about transformation as if it were decoration—something inspirational to mention at the end of a keynote, something polished to place on a website, something emotional to post after a breakthrough moment. But transformation is not decoration. It is the reason empathy and resilience matter in the first place. If empathy helps us connect and resilience helps us endure, transformation happens when connection and endurance begin to change how we live.

That is why transformation deserves its own chapter. It is not a footnote to empathy. It is not an accessory to resilience. It is the outcome that those two pillars make possible when they are practiced consistently, honestly, and with courage. If empathy is the doorway and resilience is the path, transformation is what happens when a person stops merely visiting a better future in their imagination and starts living toward it in reality.

Transformation Is More Than Change

Let us clear up a common confusion. Change and transformation are not the same thing. Change can be temporary, external, and situational. A person can change a routine, a leader can change a policy, a couple can change how often they talk, and an organization can change its language. Those changes may matter, but they do not always reach the level of transformation.

Transformation goes deeper. Transformation alters identity, meaning, and direction. It changes how a person interprets pain, how a family responds to conflict, how a leader holds power, and how a community imagines what is possible. Change adjusts behavior. Transformation reorganizes the self. Change may modify what you do. Transformation changes how you understand who you are while you are doing it.

What Transformation Looks Like in Real Life

Transformation rarely arrives with fireworks. More often, it shows up in steady, grounded decisions. It appears when a person who once lived in reactivity learns how to pause. It appears when someone who once confused survival with strength learns to receive support without shame. It appears when a leader stops using pressure as their primary tool and begins creating trust. It appears when grief no longer has the final word over a family's future, even though the grief is still real.

- I have seen transformation in soldiers who learned that vulnerability did not cancel their strength.

- I have seen it in couples who discovered that being right was costing them intimacy.
- I have seen it in highly accomplished executives who were emotionally unavailable until life forced them to confront the price of that disconnection.
- I have seen it in communities that refused to let trauma become their identity.

In every case, transformation was not magic. It was the result of honest engagement, sustained effort, and a willingness to grow beyond familiar patterns.

The Inner Work of Transformation

Transformation begins internally before it becomes visible externally. People often want new outcomes while protecting old narratives. They want peace without surrendering their resentment. They want intimacy without risking honesty. They want purpose without confronting fear. They want healing without grief. But transformation is not interested in preserving every old defense while delivering a new life. It asks for truth. It asks for responsibility. It asks for the humility to admit that some of the patterns that once protected us may now be preventing us from becoming whole.

This is where the E.R.T. Framework becomes so practical. Empathy allows a person to face themselves without immediate self-condemnation. Resilience allows that person to stay with the discomfort of growth long enough for something new to form. Then transformation begins to emerge—not because life became easy, but because the person became more grounded, more honest, and more capable of responding differently.

Transformation in Relationships

Relationships do not transform because people finally win all their arguments. They transform when people begin listening for understanding rather than ammunition. They transform when apology becomes a responsibility rather than a performance. They transform when two people stop asking, "How do I protect my position?" and start asking, "What does truth, dignity, and repair require from me now?"

In that sense, transformation is a form of relational maturity. It is what happens when empathy softens defensiveness, and resilience prevents people from running every time conflict exposes something painful. The result is not a perfect relationship. It is a more honest, more emotionally intelligent, and more sustainable one.

Transformation in Leadership and Service

The same principle applies to leadership. Plenty of leaders know how to perform competently. Fewer know how to create climates where people can trust, adapt, and grow. Transformation in leadership happens when influence becomes more than image management. It happens when a leader learns that results without humanity come at a cost, and humanity without accountability also falls short.

An empathy-driven, resilient leader does not merely manage output. That leader shapes culture. They know when to listen, when to challenge, when to recalibrate, and when to hold steady under pressure. They do not collapse in crisis, nor do they harden into emotional distance. That kind of leadership transforms teams by changing the conditions under which people work, relate, and recover.

Transformation Requires Repetition

One of the greatest myths about transformation is that it happens once and then stays fixed forever. Real transformation is strengthened by repetition. A new perspective must be practiced. A new behavior must be repeated. A healthier response must be chosen again and again until it becomes more familiar than the old defense. This is why insight alone is never enough. Insight may open the door, but practice is what teaches the body, the mind, and the relationships around us how to live differently. That is also why setbacks do not automatically mean the transformation failed. Sometimes a setback is simply evidence that growth is still becoming embodied. The question is not whether a person ever stumbles again. The question is whether they now return to truth more quickly, take responsibility more honestly, and recover with more wisdom than before. That, too, is transformation.

Why Transformation Is the Third Pillar

Transformation is the third pillar of E.R.T., as the framework is not satisfied with awareness alone. Awareness is important, but awareness without change can become sophisticated stagnation. People can learn the language of healing, leadership, and resilience without actually becoming healthier, wiser, or more responsible. Transformation is the evidence that the work has reached beneath the surface.

When empathy is present, people feel seen. When resilience is present, people can stay engaged. When transformation takes root, people begin living with greater congruence. Their choices align more closely with their values. Their leadership becomes less performative and more principled. Their relationships become less reactive and more restorative. Their suffering, while still real, no longer determines the totality of their lives.

Reflection Questions

1. Where in my life have, I confused temporary change with true transformation?
2. What old pattern, belief, or defense may be preventing deeper change in me right now?

Action Step

Identify one area where you want transformation, not just relief. Write down one repeated practice that would move you toward lasting change.

Affirmation

"I am capable of more than survival. I am willing to be transformed."

In the language of this framework, empathy tells the truth, resilience stays with the work, and transformation begins when practiced empathy and resilience reshape the way a life is lived.

PART II

The Framework in Practice

CHAPTER 5

When Empathy and Resilience Work Together

This chapter is the integration chapter of the book. The goal here is not to redefine the three pillars, but to show how they interact in lived practice. Empathy creates connection. Resilience creates capacity. Transformation emerges when connection and capacity are repeatedly applied to real circumstances. That sequence can be seen in counseling rooms, leadership settings, families, communities, and systems that are trying to grow without losing their humanity.

Before we go further, let's distinguish change from transformation. Change is often external. A company changes its logo. A person changes their diet. A school changes its curriculum. These are important, but they're not always lasting. Transformation is internal. It's when a person not only changes their behavior but their mindset, their identity, their way of being. It's when an organization not only changes policies but rewrites its culture.

Change rearranges the furniture. Transformation renovates the entire house.

That's why empathy and resilience matter. Together, they don't just produce cosmetic change. They create transformation from the inside out.

The Empathy Factor

Empathy is the spark that ignites transformation. Without empathy, people shut down. They don't feel safe enough to be vulnerable, to try, or to change.

Think of a time when you went through something painful. Maybe you lost a loved one, faced a major setback, or wrestled with self-doubt. Did someone's empathy make a difference? Did their listening, validation, or presence give you strength to move forward?

Empathy does three things:

1. **Creates Safety** – People can't transform when they feel judged. Empathy opens the door.
2. **Builds Trust** – When people feel understood, they lean into the process.
3. **Invites Honesty** – Empathy gives people permission to tell the truth about their struggles.

Transformation starts with the courage to face reality, and empathy makes that possible.

The Resilience Factor

If empathy is the spark, resilience is the fuel. Empathy opens the door, but resilience walks us through it.

Resilience is the capacity to recover from setbacks, adapt to change, and keep moving toward growth even when life knocks us down. Without resilience, empathy can become overwhelming. You can care deeply about others, but if you don't have the strength to sustain the work, you burn out.

Resilience keeps transformation going when the excitement wears off and the challenges show up. It's what allows a person to continue therapy after the initial breakthrough. It's what helps a leader push through resistance when implementing a new vision. It's what helps a community rebuild after tragedy.

Resilience does three things:

1. **Provides Strength** – It helps people stay the course when things get hard.
2. **Builds Adaptability** – It allows people to pivot rather than break under pressure.
3. **Generates Hope** – Resilience reminds us that setbacks are not the end of the story.

Why Empathy Alone Falls Short

I've met incredible professionals—social workers, teachers, healthcare providers—who were overflowing with empathy. They could sit with someone's pain, validate their experience, and offer deep compassion. But many of them struggled with burnout. Why? Because empathy without resilience drains you.

Empathy opens you to the suffering of others. Without resilience, you absorb it and can't recover. You can end up overwhelmed, exhausted, and unable to continue the work you're called to do. That's why empathy alone cannot sustain transformation. It ignites the process but needs resilience to carry it forward.

Why Resilience Alone Falls Short

On the other hand, resilience without empathy is equally incomplete. I've seen leaders who were tough, focused, and highly adaptable. They could weather storms and keep pushing forward. But their lack of empathy created toxic environments. Their teams didn't feel seen or valued. Their organizations survived, but they didn't thrive.

Resilience without empathy produces cold survival, not transformation. It gets you through, but it doesn't connect you to others. It builds walls instead of bridges. That's why resilience alone cannot create transformation. It provides strength, but without empathy, it misses humanity.

Together, They Create Transformation

When empathy and resilience come together, something powerful happens.

- Empathy softens resilience so it doesn't become cold.
- Resilience strengthens empathy, so it doesn't become fragile.

Together, they produce a transformation that is both human and sustainable.

Let me give you some examples.

Example #1: Transformation in Counseling

A young woman came to me struggling with grief after losing her father. She felt stuck, as if life had ended with his passing.

Empathy allowed me to enter her pain with her. I didn't rush her past her grief. I sat with her in it. That created safety and trust.

Then, resilience helped us build a path forward. We worked on small steps: getting out of bed, re-engaging with school, and finding ways to honor her father's memory. Over time, she discovered that her loss didn't have to define her story. She could carry her father's legacy while still creating her own future.

That was transformation.

Example #2: Transformation in Leadership

I once worked with a corporate manager whose team had disengaged. She was driving hard for results, but her employees were burnt out and resentful.

When I introduced empathy, she began to listen differently. She asked her team, "What's one thing I could do to make your work easier?" That single question opened the floodgates. Her team began to trust her again.

But empathy alone wouldn't fix the system. She also needed resilience to navigate the pushback from higher leadership when she advocated for her team. She had to adapt policies, restructure workloads, and endure criticism. Empathy rebuilt relationships. Resilience sustained change. Together, they transformed her leadership.

Examples #3: Transformation in Community

In a community devastated by violence, people felt hopeless. Empathy was needed first—spaces for people to share their grief, anger, and fear. That collective empathy created solidarity. People realized they weren't alone.

Then resilience kicked in. Leaders and residents came together to design youth programs, rebuild public spaces, and advocate for safer policies. The process wasn't easy, but resilience carried them through setbacks.

The result? A community that didn't just heal but began to thrive again.

The Equation in Practice

Here's the formula simplified:

- Empathy creates connection. People feel seen, heard, and valued.
- Resilience creates strength. People find the capacity to recover and adapt.

Together, they create transformation. Lasting change that goes deeper than surface adjustments.

Reflection Questions

1. Where in your life have you relied too much on empathy without resilience?
2. Where have you leaned on resilience without empathy?
3. What transformation might happen if you combined the two?
4. Where have I practiced empathy without resilience—or resilience without empathy?
5. What transformation could happen if I intentionally combined both?

Closing Inspiration

Transformation is not reserved for a select few. It is available to anyone willing to embrace both empathy and resilience.

- **Empathy says**, "I will connect with your humanity."
- **Resilience says**, "I will not give up when life gets hard."
- **Together, they say,** "We will be transformed."

This is not just theory. It's the blueprint for change in families, organizations, and communities. It's the heartbeat of the E.R.T. Framework™.

Action Step

Choose one area of your life and apply both empathy and resilience this week.

Affirmation

"When empathy meets resilience, transformation becomes inevitable."

CHAPTER 6

The Five-Step Model

Practicing the E.R.T. Framework

A framework becomes truly useful when it can be practiced in a repeatable way. The Five-Step Model translates empathy, resilience, and transformation from concept into method so that individuals, helpers, leaders, and systems can move from intention to disciplined application.

Why a Model Matters

Empathy and resilience are powerful concepts, but without structure, they can remain abstract. People ask me all the time: "How do I actually practice empathy? How do I build resilience in a real situation?"

That's why I created the **Five-Step Model**—a roadmap that translates the philosophy of empathy and resilience into action. Whether you are a social worker, leader, counselor, coach, or community organizer, this model gives you a way to live out the approach in your daily work.

The model is simple enough to remember but deep enough to guide transformation at the individual, family, organizational, and community levels.

The steps are:

1. Engage with Empathy
2. Assess Through a Resilience Lens
3. Co-Create Pathways for Change
4. Deliver with Empathy-Driven Tools
5. Evaluate for Transformation

Let's walk through each one.

Step 1: Engage with Empathy

Transformation begins with connection. Before you can help someone grow, heal, or change, they must feel understood. Engagement is not about convincing someone or impressing them with credentials. It's about presence.

What this looks like:

- Active listening without judgment
- Asking open-ended questions
- Showing genuine curiosity about the person's experience
- Naming and validating emotions

Story:
While working with inner-city youth in a mentoring program, I met with a teenager who was labeled "difficult" by the youth counselors. Instead of lecturing him about responsibility, I asked, "What's the hardest part

of your day?" His answer opened my eyes to the challenges he faced at home—things his counselors had never considered. That moment of empathy changed how we engaged moving forward.

Reflection Question:
When was the last time you slowed down to truly engage with someone's story before offering advice?

Step 2: Assess Through a Resilience Lens

Traditional assessments often focus on deficits: what's wrong, what's missing, what's broken. While it's important to identify challenges, the E.R.T. Framework™ also emphasizes assessing resilience—what strengths, coping skills, and support systems are already present.

What this looks like:

Asking, "How have you coped with challenges in the past?"

- Identifying strengths alongside struggles
- Mapping out personal and community resources
- Looking for patterns of adaptation, not just patterns of failure

Story:
A family I worked with had been through multiple crises—job loss, eviction, health struggles. On paper, it looked like endless deficits. But when I asked them how they managed to stay together, they told me about family dinners they held no matter what, and their strong faith community. Naming those strengths gave them confidence to keep moving forward.

Reflection Question:
How might your perspective shift if you assessed people not only by their problems, but also by their resilience?

Step 3: Co-Create Pathways for Change

Too often, solutions are imposed on people from the outside. But real transformation happens when people are empowered to design their own pathways. Co-creation means walking alongside, not dragging or dictating.

What this looks like:
Collaboratively setting goals (SMARTIE goals: Specific, Measurable, Achievable, Relevant, Time-bound, Inclusive, and Equitable)

Asking, "What do you want to see change, and how can we work toward that together?"

- Balancing professional expertise with the client's lived experience
- Ensuring ownership of the process remains with the individual or community

Story:
During a leadership training, I asked participants to develop action steps to improve communication in their teams. Instead of me handing them a template, we built it together based on their realities. The result? A plan that was more effective because it was theirs.

Reflection Question:
When was the last time you invited those you serve to co-create solutions rather than follow your blueprint?

Step 4: Deliver with Empathy-Driven Tools

Engagement, assessment, and co-creation are powerful, but at some point, action must be taken. Delivery is about implementing strategies, interventions, and tools that are grounded in empathy and resilience.

What this looks like:

- Counseling sessions that use trauma-informed care
- Coaching conversations that balance challenge with compassion
- Leadership strategies that prioritize people over productivity
- Organizational consulting that embeds equity into systems

Story:
At Walter Reed, our resilience program wasn't just about stress management techniques. It was about equipping military members with tools rooted in empathy—like peer support systems—so they didn't feel alone. The tools worked because they addressed both the human and the structural side of resilience.

Reflection Question:
Do the tools you deliver reinforce empathy and resilience, or do they unintentionally undermine them?

Step 5: Evaluate for Transformation

Many programs stop at delivery. But without evaluation, you don't know if transformation has actually occurred. Evaluation in the E.R.T. Framework™ is not just about checking boxes. It's about asking: Has empathy deepened? Has resilience strengthened? Has transformation occurred?

What this looks like:
Collecting both quantitative (surveys, data) and qualitative (stories, feedback) evidence.

- Asking participants to reflect on their growth in empathy and resilience

- Identifying what worked, what didn't, and what needs adjustment
- Celebrating progress, not just perfection

Story:
One organization I worked with wanted to measure success purely by productivity. After integrating empathy and resilience into their leadership model, we evaluated them differently. We looked at employee engagement, retention, and workplace morale. Those indicators showed transformation that traditional metrics would have missed.

Reflection Question:
Are you measuring transformation, or just activity?

The Five Steps as a Cycle

These steps are not one-and-done. They form a cycle. You engage, assess, co-create, deliver, and evaluate—and then you start again, building deeper levels of empathy, resilience, and transformation with each round.

Closing Inspiration

The Five-Step Model is more than a framework. It's a way of working, leading, and living. It reminds us that empathy without resilience is fragile, and resilience without empathy is cold. Together, they create transformation—but only when we put them into practice.

When you engage with empathy, assess through a resilience lens, co-create pathways for change, deliver with empathy-driven tools, and evaluate for transformation, you don't just change outcomes. You change lives. And that is the heart of the E.R.T. Framework™.

Reflection Questions

1. Which of the five steps comes most naturally to me? Which is hardest?
2. How might following these steps help me in my current challenges?

Action Step

Apply the Five-Step Model to one personal or professional situation this week.

Affirmation

"I can walk step by step toward transformation."

CHAPTER 7

Core Values of the E.R.T. Approach

Values answer the question, "How do we operate?" They are not slogans. They are the operational commitments that shape how the E.R.T. Framework™ is practiced in leadership, counseling, community work, coaching, and service.

Why Values Matter

Every approach, every organization, every leader is ultimately guided by values—whether they name them or not. Values act as the compass that points us toward what matters most when circumstances get confusing. Without clear values, empathy becomes sentiment, and resilience becomes stubbornness. But when empathy and resilience are anchored in values, they become powerful tools for transformation.

That's why the E.R.T. Framework™ is built on five core values:

1. Integrity
2. Inclusion
3. Empowerment
4. Community
5. Hope

These are not just words on a wall. They are lived commitments.

Let's walk through each one.

1. Integrity – Walking in Truth

Integrity is about alignment—living in a way that matches your words with your actions, your values with your decisions, your character with your leadership.

In counseling, integrity means being transparent with clients and honoring ethical guidelines. In coaching, it means telling the truth even when it's uncomfortable. In leadership, it means making decisions that serve people, not just profits.

Story:
I once consulted with a nonprofit leader who admitted, "We have diversity on paper, but not in practice." It took integrity to say that out loud. Once she did, we were able to design real equity strategies. Integrity wasn't about perfection—it was about honesty.

Reflection Question:
Where in your work or life do you need to realign your actions with your values?

2. Inclusion – Creating Space for All

Inclusion is more than representation—it's about belonging. It's about creating spaces where people don't just show up but feel like they truly matter.

Inclusion recognizes that empathy without action is incomplete. We must not only listen to marginalized voices but also restructure systems so that those voices have power.

Story:
During a training, I asked participants to share a time they felt excluded. The stories ranged from childhood bullying to workplace discrimination. As people shared, you could feel the empathy in the room deepen. But then I asked, "What policies or practices might prevent those exclusions from happening again?" That's where inclusion moves from emotion to transformation.

Reflection Question:
How do you move from inviting people to the table to actually giving them a voice at the table?

3. Empowerment – Unlocking Potential

Empowerment is about helping people discover that they already have strength within them. It's not about rescuing—it's about equipping.

In therapy, empowerment means showing clients that they are not defined by their trauma. In coaching, it means asking questions that unlock hidden potential. In leadership, it means developing people rather than controlling them.

Story:

I once coached a young professional who kept saying, "I'm not ready for leadership." Instead of convincing him otherwise, I asked, "What evidence do you already have that you are leading?" As he named examples—mentoring colleagues, volunteering in the community—his perspective shifted. He realized he was already leading, just without the title.

That's empowerment.

Reflection Question:

When you support others, are you rescuing them or empowering them?

4. Community – We Rise Together

No one transforms alone. Community multiplies empathy and resilience. It's in relationships, families, organizations, and neighborhoods where transformation becomes sustainable.

Community reminds us that resilience is not just individual toughness—it's collective strength.

Story:

When I served in the military, I saw firsthand how community fueled resilience. Soldiers could face extraordinary challenges because they knew they weren't facing them alone. The bond of "we're in this together" was stronger than any obstacle.

Reflection Question:

How do you intentionally build communities of support in your work and life?

5. Hope – Fuel for the Future

Finally, hope. Hope is not wishful thinking—it's the belief that the future can be better than the present, and the commitment to work toward it.

Empathy without hope leads to despair. Resilience without hope leads to survival mode. But empathy and resilience fueled by hope lead to transformation.

Story:
I worked with a community that had faced generational poverty. Many residents felt nothing would ever change. But when we introduced small wins—youth programs, mentorship opportunities, job readiness training—hope began to return. You could see it in their posture, their energy, their willingness to dream again. Hope transformed survival into thriving.

Living the Values

These five values—integrity, inclusion, empowerment, community, and hope—are not just concepts. They are practices. They show up in the way you speak to a client, design a program, lead a meeting, or respond to conflict.

When these values guide empathy and resilience, the result is transformation that lasts.

Closing Inspiration

The core values of the E.R.T. Framework™ are more than ideals—they are commitments. They remind us that empathy must be honest (integrity), inclusive (inclusion), empowering (empowerment), communal (community), and forward-looking (hope).

When you anchor your life and work in these values, empathy and resilience don't just change situations; they change people. They transform people, organizations, and communities from the inside out.

Reflection Questions

1. Which core value (integrity, inclusion, empowerment, community, hope) resonates most with me?
2. Where in my life do I need to realign with these values?
3. Where do you need to hold onto hope in your own journey?

Action Step

Pick one value and create a practical way to live it out this week.

Affirmation

"My values anchor my empathy, resilience, and transformation."

CHAPTER 8

What We Believe About People, Healing, and Growth

If values describe how we operate, beliefs describe what anchors us. These beliefs are the deeper truths about people, healing, leadership, dignity, and growth that give the framework its direction.

Why Beliefs Matter

Every movement begins with belief. Beliefs shape behavior. Behavior shapes culture. And culture shapes destiny.

The E.R.T. Framework™ is not just a framework. It is a way of seeing, a way of acting, a way of living. At its core, it rests on a set of deeply held beliefs that anchor every counseling session, coaching conversation, consulting strategy, keynote message, and leadership decision. These are not abstract ideals. They are convictions tested in the crucible of real life. They come from military bases, therapy offices, corporate boardrooms, community meetings, and personal journeys through adversity.

And so, here is what we believe.

We Believe in the Power of Empathy

- We believe that empathy is more than a soft skill. It is a human necessity. Without empathy, people feel unseen and unheard. With empathy, they feel valued and connected.
- We believe empathy is the foundation of trust in every relationship.
- We believe empathy has the power to dismantle prejudice, build bridges, and heal divides.
- We believe empathy is not weakness but strength—the courage to step into another's world without losing your own.

We Believe in the Strength of Resilience

- We believe resilience is more than "toughing it out." It is the art of rising, adapting, and thriving even in the face of adversity.
- We believe resilience is not just for individuals but for families, organizations, and communities.
- We believe resilience is built, not inherited. It grows through challenge, reflection, and support.
- We believe resilience turns setbacks into comebacks and pain into purpose.

We Believe in Transformation

- We believe transformation is possible—for individuals stuck in cycles of trauma, for organizations trapped in toxic cultures, for communities burdened by inequity.

- We believe transformation happens when empathy and resilience meet.
- We believe transformation is deeper than change; it rewrites identity, purpose, and possibility.
- We believe transformation is not an event but a journey, marked by small steps and courageous choices.

We Believe in Integrity

- We believe in speaking the truth, even when it costs.
- We believe words and actions must align.
- We believe integrity is the bedrock of trust, without which empathy and resilience cannot flourish.

We Believe in Inclusion

- We believe every person has a seat at the table and a voice worth hearing.
- We believe inclusion is not charity; it is justice.
- We believe empathy without equity is incomplete.

We Believe in Empowerment

- We believe people are not problems to be fixed but potentials to be unlocked.
- We believe empowerment equips people to stand on their own, not depend on rescue.
- We believe true leadership multiplies leaders, not followers.

We Believe in Community

- We believe no one rises alone.
- We believe community is where empathy and resilience multiply.
- We believe strong communities are built not on perfection but on shared humanity.

We Believe in Hope

- We believe hope is oxygen for the soul.
- We believe hope is not naïve but radical—choosing to see light in the darkest places.
- We believe hope transforms survival into thriving.

We Believe in Action

- We believe empathy without action is sentiment.
- We believe resilience without application is survival mode.
- We believe belief without action is empty.

That is why the E.R.T. Framework™ calls us not only to feel and endure but to transform—ourselves, our organizations, our communities, and our world.

Closing Declaration

This is our manifesto.

This is what we believe.

This is who we are.

If you align with these beliefs, then you are already part of the movement. Whether you are a student, a leader, a parent, a counselor, or a neighbor, you can live the E.R.T. Framework™. And when you do, you won't just change outcomes. You'll change lives.

Reflection Questions

1. Which belief from this chapter do I already live by?
2. Which belief do I need to embrace more fully?

Action Step

Share one of the beliefs from this chapter with a friend, colleague, or family member and discuss it.

Affirmation

"What I believe shapes how I live and lead."

PART III

E.R.T. in Action

CHAPTER 9

Human Services Delivery

Human services work is strongest when it resists both cold bureaucracy and exhausted overextension. The E.R.T. Framework™ improves service delivery by strengthening relational trust, reducing burnout risk, and helping systems become more responsive to the actual lives of the people they serve.

Human Services at a Crossroads

Human services professionals are among the most dedicated people I know. They are social workers, case managers, nonprofit leaders, youth advocates, community organizers, and counselors. They step into the messiest, most complex situations: poverty, trauma, abuse, homelessness, family conflict, systemic inequities. And they do it not for fame or fortune, but because they care about people.

But let's be honest—human services are at a crossroads. Burnout rates are high. Funding is tight. Caseloads are overwhelming. Too often, the work feels reactive rather than proactive. That's why a new approach is needed. Not another policy manual or another checklist, but a way of working that restores the human spirit—both for the professional and for the client.

The E.R.T. Framework™ offers a new way to embed empathy and resilience into every layer of human services so transformation becomes possible.

Shifting from Deficit-Based to Strengths-Based

Traditionally, human services have been deficit-focused:

1. What's wrong with the client?
2. What's broken in the family?
3. What resources are missing in the community?

While identifying needs is important, staying stuck in deficits can unintentionally reinforce disempowerment. Clients begin to see themselves as problems to be fixed rather than people with potential. Workers feel like firefighters constantly putting out flames instead of cultivators helping growth take root.

The E.R.T. Framework™ flips the script. It says:

1. What resilience has this client already shown?
2. What strengths exist in this family system?
3. What community assets can we build on?

This doesn't ignore the struggles—it reframes them to highlight possibility.

Story:
I once worked with a family facing eviction. On paper, they looked like another "high-risk case." But when I asked them how they had managed to stay together despite constant stress, they told me about weekly family dinners they refused to give up. That dinner ritual was their resilience. Naming it helped them realize they had more stability than they thought. From there, we built strategies that tapped into that resilience.

Trauma-Informed Care Through Empathy and Resilience

One of the biggest shifts in human services over the last two decades has been the move toward trauma-informed care. We now know that many of the behaviors professionals encounter—anger, withdrawal, aggression, mistrust—are often rooted in trauma.

The E.R.T. Framework™ complements this shift perfectly. Trauma-informed care asks: "What happened to you?" instead of "What's wrong with you?" Empathy deepens that question by listening without judgment. Resilience expands it by asking: "How have you survived, and how can you thrive?"

Example:
A teenager constantly skipped school. Instead of labeling him "truant," I used empathy to learn his story. His family was unstable, and he often missed school to care for younger siblings. Then, through resilience, we explored how he had developed leadership and caregiving skills at such a young age. That reframe empowered him to see himself not as a failure but as a leader in training.

Supporting the Worker, Not Just the Client

Here's a truth we often avoid: human service workers are human, too. They carry secondary trauma, compassion fatigue, and the stress of navigating broken systems. Without support, empathy can wear them down. That's why the E.R.T. Framework™ is designed not just for clients but also for workers. It gives professionals tools for self-care, emotional regulation, peer support, and resilience-building.

When workers practice empathy for themselves and resilience in their routines, they can sustain their calling rather than burn out.

Practice Tip:

Start supervision meetings with a resilience check-in: "What's one way you took care of yourself this week?"

1. Normalize conversations about emotional strain.
2. Model resilience at the organizational level by promoting manageable caseloads, professional development, and wellness practices.

Building Trust in Communities

One of the greatest challenges in human services is distrust. Many clients have been let down by systems—schools, hospitals, courts, agencies. Why should they trust another professional?

- Empathy is the bridge. Resilience is the follow-through.
- Empathy builds initial trust: "I see you. I'm not here to judge."
- Resilience proves commitment: "I'll keep showing up even when it's hard."

When communities see professionals consistently combine empathy and resilience, skepticism turns into trust. Trust becomes the foundation for transformation.

Story:
In Baltimore, I worked with a community organization serving youth impacted by violence. At first, many teenagers were skeptical. They'd seen programs come and go. But after several months of consistent engagement, they said, "You didn't give up on us like the others." That was resilience in action—and it built lasting trust.

Applications in Human Services Settings

Let's look at how the Five-Step Model (from Chapter 5) applies specifically to human services:

1. **Engage with Empathy** – Begin every intake with presence, not paperwork.
2. **Assess Through a Resilience Lens** – Identify coping strategies, community supports, and strengths.
3. **Co-Create Pathways for Change** – Let clients set goals alongside professionals.
4. **Deliver with Empathy-Driven Tools** – Provide interventions that honor dignity and build capacity.
5. **Evaluate for Transformation** – Measure not only services delivered but lives impacted.

From Surviving to Thriving

Ultimately, the goal of human services is not just to help people survive—it's to help them thrive. Surviving means getting through the day. Thriving means building a life of dignity, purpose, and joy.

Empathy helps people believe they matter. Resilience helps them believe they can make it. Together, they move people beyond survival into thriving.

Closing Inspiration

Human services work is sacred work. It is often messy, exhausting, and underappreciated. But it is also where some of the most profound transformations take place.

When empathy and resilience guide human services, people no longer feel like case numbers. They feel like human beings with dignity and potential. Workers no longer feel like cogs in a system. They feel like change agents. Communities no longer feel forgotten. They feel seen, supported, and strengthened. This is what happens when we deliver human services through the E.R.T. Framework™. It's not just service delivery. It's transformation delivery.

Reflection Questions

1. Do I focus more on deficits or strengths when serving others?
2. How can I bring more empathy into my professional or community role?
3. Do I see my clients through a deficit lens or a resilience lens?
4. How do I practice empathy not only for clients but for myself and my colleagues?
5. In what ways does my work empower people to thrive rather than just survive?

Action Step

Identify one client, colleague, or neighbor and affirm their resilience out loud.

Affirmation

"I serve best when I see both the struggle and the strength."

CHAPTER 10

Serving Military Members and Veterans

This chapter honors the distinct realities of military life while remaining relevant to the broader reader. Service, trauma, transition, family strain, and identity all require an approach that can hold discipline and humanity at the same time.

Honoring Those Who Serve

When you raise your right hand and swear an oath to serve, you join a tradition bigger than yourself. You wear a uniform that carries history, sacrifice, and responsibility. For military members and veterans, service shapes identity. It forges resilience but often demands more than any human should have to give.

Serving those who serve is both an honor and a responsibility. Military members and veterans are not statistics. They are fathers, mothers, sons, daughters, leaders, neighbors. They carry unique strengths—and unique wounds. That's why they need more than generic services. They need an approach that honors their sacrifice, validates their humanity, and equips them to thrive beyond survival. That's exactly what the E.R.T. Framework™ offers.

The Invisible Wounds

We often think of military service in terms of physical strength, discipline, and courage. And those qualities are real. But beneath the surface, many carry invisible wounds:

Trauma from combat or training accidents

- Moral injury from witnessing or participating in ethically challenging situations
- Loss from separation, death of comrades, or fractured relationships
- Identity struggles when transitioning from military to civilian life.
- Empathy helps us see these wounds. Resilience equips us to heal them.

Why Empathy Matters for Military Members

Military culture often emphasizes toughness. Phrases like "suck it up" or "drive on" are meant to build grit—but they can also silence pain. That's where empathy becomes revolutionary.

Empathy says:

- "Your experiences are valid."
- "Your feelings don't make you weak—they make you human."

- "You don't have to carry this alone."

When I worked with service members at Walter Reed, the most common thing they said wasn't, "I want advice." It was, "I just need someone who understands."

Empathy was often the first step to healing.

Why Resilience Matters for Veterans

Resilience is woven into military life. Training pushes limits. Deployments test adaptability. Service demands perseverance. But resilience in service doesn't always translate to resilience after service.

Transitioning to civilian life can feel like entering a different world. The structure is gone. The mission is unclear. The sense of belonging fades. Veterans may feel resilient in combat but vulnerable in everyday civilian challenges. That's why resilience must be reframed: not just about pushing through hardship, but about adapting, growing, and thriving in new environments.

Resilience says:

- "I can use the strength I built in service to succeed in civilian life."
- "Setbacks don't erase my skills—they reveal new ways to use them."
- "My story isn't over; it's evolving."

Lessons from Walter Reed

From 2012 to 2016, I had the privilege of serving as Chief of Resilience and Psychological Services at Walter Reed National Military Medical

Center. In that role, I saw both the incredible strength and the deep pain of service members and families.

What made the difference in outcomes wasn't just medical treatment or policy changes—it was empathy and resilience in action.

1. **Empathy:** listening to soldiers' stories without judgment, creating safe spaces to grieve, and validating the complexity of their emotions.
2. **Resilience:** equipping them with skills to regulate emotions, rebuild identity, and envision life beyond the uniform.

Our program became recognized as a best practice not because it had fancy resources, but because it combined empathy and resilience in every interaction.

The E.R.T. Framework™ in Action with Veterans

Here's how the Five-Step Model applies to military members and veterans:

1. **Engage with Empathy** – Acknowledge the sacrifice. Listen deeply to stories of deployment, loss, or transition.
2. **Assess Through a Resilience Lens** – Identify the skills already developed in service (discipline, teamwork, adaptability) and apply them to new challenges.
3. **Co-Create Pathways for Change** – Design transition plans that honor military identity while building civilian purpose.
4. **Deliver with Empathy-Driven Tools** – Provide trauma-informed counseling, peer support groups, and resilience training.
5. **Evaluate for Transformation** – Look for signs of thriving: restored relationships, meaningful careers, renewed hope.

Stories of Transformation

The Veteran Who Found His Mission Again: A former Marine felt lost after leaving the Corps. Through empathy, we explored his grief over losing the structure and brotherhood. Through resilience, we identified his leadership skills and connected him with a nonprofit role serving at-risk youth. He found purpose again—not in uniform, but in mission.

The Family That Rebuilt Together: A soldier returning from deployment struggled with anger outbursts at home. Empathy gave his spouse space to express her hurt. Resilience equipped both of them with communication tools and coping strategies. Their marriage didn't just survive—it grew stronger.

The Wounded Warrior Who Redefined Strength: A soldier who lost a limb in combat told me, "I'll never be strong again." Empathy allowed me to sit in his grief. Resilience reframed his story: his strength wasn't gone—it was being expressed differently. He later became a mentor to other wounded warriors.

Why This Matters Beyond the Military

The lessons of serving military members and veterans ripple outward. They remind us that:

- People are more than their roles or uniforms.
- Healing requires both empathy and resilience.
- Transitions, whether military or civilian, always require support.

In serving military members, we learn lessons about humanity that apply to everyone.

Closing Inspiration

Serving military members and veterans is sacred work. They served for something larger than themselves. Our role is to give back—not with pity, but with empathy. Not with quick fixes, but with resilience.

When empathy and resilience guide our work, military members feel honored, veterans feel equipped, and families feel supported. Transformation becomes possible—not just survival but thriving. This is what it means to serve those who have served—through the E.R.T. Framework™—Empathy, Resilience and Transformation.

Reflection Questions

1. What sacrifices have I overlooked in the lives of military members or veterans I know?
2. How can I show empathy and respect for their resilience?
3. Do I honor the unique strengths and struggles of military members and veterans, or do I treat them as just another client group?
4. How can I integrate empathy into my work with service members without undermining their resilience?
5. What resilience structures can I help veterans build for life beyond service?

Action Step

Reach out to a veteran or service member this week with gratitude and support.

Affirmation

"Honoring service means meeting it with empathy and resilience."

CHAPTER 11

Social Justice and Anti-Racism Work

Justice work cannot be sustained by outrage alone. It requires empathy that refuses dehumanization, resilience that resists burnout, and transformation that pushes beyond performance into principled change.

Why Social Justice Requires More Than Outrage

Social justice has become one of the most urgent conversations of our time. We hear about racial inequities, systemic oppression, and cultural divides almost daily. And yet, despite awareness campaigns, hashtags, and corporate pledges, real change often feels painfully slow.

Why? Because awareness without empathy becomes shallow. And outrage without resilience burns out. That's why the E.R.T. Framework™ matters in social justice work. It reminds us that sustainable change requires two things:

1. Empathy to humanize those who have been dehumanized.
2. Resilience to keep pushing when the system resists, when fatigue sets in, when progress feels invisible.

Empathy in Social Justice

At its core, injustice thrives on dehumanization. Labels replace names. Stereotypes replace stories. People become "othered."

- Empathy disrupts this process. It forces us to slow down and see the person behind the label.
- Empathy listens to the lived experiences of marginalized communities without defensiveness.
- Empathy validates pain instead of dismissing it.
- Empathy creates bridges between groups who might otherwise remain divided.

Story:
During a training on allyship, a white executive said, "I never realized how exhausting it is for my Black colleagues to constantly prove their worth." That realization didn't come from statistics—it came from listening empathetically to coworkers' stories.

Empathy is often the first crack in the wall of indifference.

Resilience in Social Justice

But empathy alone is not enough. Social justice is not a sprint. It is a marathon across generations. Without resilience, advocates burn out. Communities lose hope. Movements fizzle.

Resilience allows us to:

1. Stay engaged even when progress is slow.
2. Rebound after setbacks, policy defeats, or public backlash.
3. Protect mental health while still pushing for systemic change.

Example:
The Civil Rights Movement was not sustained by empathy alone. It was sustained by resilience—marching after being beaten, organizing after being jailed, voting after being threatened. Empathy fueled compassion. Resilience fueled endurance. Together, they transformed a nation.

Why Awareness Isn't Enough

Today, we live in an age of awareness. Social media can spread information globally in minutes.

But awareness is only the first step. Real transformation requires empathy and resilience.

- Awareness says: "I see the problem."
- Empathy says: "I feel the pain of those affected."
- Resilience says, "I will keep working until justice is done."

Without empathy, awareness becomes performative. Without resilience, awareness becomes temporary. With both, awareness becomes transformation.

Applying the Five-Step Model to Social Justice

The E.R. Doctor Five-Step Model provides a roadmap for justice work:

1. **Engage with Empathy** – Listen to marginalized voices. Center lived experiences.

2. **Assess Through a Resilience Lens** – Identify strengths within oppressed communities, not just struggles.
3. **Co-Create Pathways for Change** – Work alongside communities, not on their behalf. Shared power, not charity.
4. **Deliver with Empathy-Driven Tools** – Policies and practices that humanize, not dehumanize.
5. **Evaluate for Transformation** – Are inequities being dismantled? Are communities thriving, not just surviving?

Moving Beyond Performative Allyship

One of the greatest dangers in social justice work is performative allyship—saying the right things without changing anything.

The E.R.T. Framework™ challenges us to:

- Move from statements to systems.
- Move from charity to equity.
- Move from temporary outrage to sustained resilience.

Story:
A company once asked me to train its executives after a high-profile racial incident. They wanted a "quick fix." I told them, "This isn't about a workshop. It's about reshaping culture." Empathy helped them hear employees' pain. Resilience helped them commit to long-term systemic changes.

Healing Communities Through Empathy and Resilience

Communities facing systemic oppression don't just need justice—they need healing. Empathy acknowledges the wounds. Resilience helps communities build strength to thrive despite them.

- Empathy validates trauma caused by racism and inequity.
- Resilience equips communities with skills, support networks, and resources to rise.

Closing Inspiration

Justice without empathy becomes harsh. Justice without resilience becomes fragile. But justice with both empathy and resilience becomes unstoppable.

Social justice and anti-racism work require courage, consistency, and conviction. The E.R.T. Framework™ equips us with the tools to sustain the fight, not just for awareness, but for transformation. Because at the end of the day, justice is not just about systems—it's about people. And people thrive when empathy and resilience come together.

Reflection Questions

1. When have I witnessed injustice, and how did I respond?
2. What resilience practices will sustain me if I commit to justice work?
3. Together, they create justice that is not only legal but also lived.
4. Do I listen to marginalized voices with empathy, or do I filter them through my own assumptions?
5. How am I building resilience to stay engaged in justice work in the long term?
6. In my organization, are we measuring progress by activity (statements, trainings) or transformation (policy, culture, equity)?

Action Step

Take one small step toward justice this week—sign a petition, join a conversation, or support a marginalized voice.

Affirmation

"Justice rooted in empathy and resilience cannot be stopped."

CHAPTER 12

Merit-Based Hiring and Leadership

Hiring and leadership systems are healthiest when they combine fairness, discernment, and humanity. In the E.R.T. Framework™, empathy improves how people are seen, resilience improves how systems respond under pressure, and transformation improves the culture those systems produce.

Why the Way We Hire Matters

Every organization says its people are its greatest asset. Yet, the way many organizations hire and promote people tells a different story. Hiring often reflects bias, favoritism, and superficial measures of success—like where someone went to school or who they know—instead of true merit.

The result? Talented candidates get overlooked. Employees feel undervalued. Leadership becomes a title instead of a trust.

The E.R.T. Framework™ offers a new way forward: one that anchors hiring and leadership in empathy and resilience. This approach ensures organizations don't just fill positions—they build cultures where people can thrive.

What Is Merit-Based Hiring?

At its core, merit-based hiring means evaluating candidates on their skills, abilities, and potential rather than irrelevant or biased factors. But under this approach, merit isn't defined narrowly. It's not just about technical skills.

True merit includes:

1. Competence – skills and knowledge for the role.
2. Character – integrity, accountability, and ethics.
3. Capacity – resilience, adaptability, and growth potential.
4. Connection – empathy, communication, and awareness of inclusion.

When organizations adopt this holistic definition of merit, they open the door to stronger, fairer, and more resilient workplaces.

Why Empathy Matters in Hiring

Hiring isn't just about selecting the best candidate—it's about creating an equitable process that respects human dignity.

Empathy in hiring means:

- Writing inclusive job postings that invite diverse candidates.
- Listening to applicants' stories instead of reducing them to résumés.

- Considering the barriers people have overcome as evidence of resilience.
- Giving clear, respectful feedback, whether someone is hired or not.

Story:
I once worked for a company that dismissed candidates with employment gaps. When I encouraged them to ask why, they learned that one candidate had taken time to care for a terminally ill parent. That experience had given her resilience, adaptability, and compassion—qualities that made her an even stronger leader.

Empathy revealed her true value.

Why Resilience Matters in Hiring

Resilience is one of the most important predictors of long-term success in any role. Technical skills may get someone hired, but resilience keeps them thriving when challenges come.

Resilience in hiring means looking for evidence of:

- Overcoming setbacks in personal or professional life.
- Adapting to change without losing focus.
- Turning failures into lessons learned.
- Demonstrating persistence in pursuit of goals.

Story:
In one interview panel, a candidate was asked about their proudest achievement. Instead of citing a typical career highlight, they shared how they rebuilt their career after being laid off during a recession. That story showed not just skill but resilience. The organization later said it was the best hire they had made in years.

Leadership Through the E.R.T. Framework™

Leadership is not about authority. It's about influence, trust, and transformation. The best leaders are those who combine empathy with resilience. Empathy in leadership means listening, validating, and understanding your people. Resilience in leadership means navigating uncertainty, making tough decisions, and modeling adaptability. Together, they create leaders who inspire—not through fear or power, but through connection and courage.

The Five-Step Model in Hiring & Leadership

Here's how the E.R. Doctor Five-Step Model applies:

1. **Engage with Empathy** – See candidates and employees as people, not just roles.
2. **Assess Through a Resilience Lens** – Evaluate potential based on adaptability and problem-solving, not just credentials.
3. **Co-Create Pathways for Growth** – Partner with employees to design career paths that align with their strengths and aspirations.
4. **Deliver with Empathy-Driven Leadership** – Create policies and practices that build trust and dignity.
5. **Evaluate for Transformation** – Measure leadership not only by productivity but by engagement, inclusion, and thriving teams.

Moving Beyond Bias

Bias is one of the greatest threats to merit-based hiring. Whether conscious or unconscious, biases often lead to unfair decisions. The E.R.T. Framework™ disrupts bias by using structured interviews with clear rubrics, training hiring panels in empathy and resilience awareness, asking questions that reveal character and capacity, not just credentials and creating accountability in decision-making.

Closing Inspiration

Hiring and leadership are not just organizational tasks—they are moral responsibilities. The people you hire and the way you lead shape your organization's culture, values, and future.

When empathy and resilience guide those decisions, merit rises to the top, bias fades to the background, and transformation becomes the norm. This is what happens when we hire and lead through the E.R.T. Framework™. We don't just build teams—we build thriving, resilient, and just workplaces.

Reflection Questions for Leaders

1. Do I define merit narrowly (skills, credentials) or holistically (skills + character + resilience + empathy)?
2. How does empathy show up in the way my organization recruits, hires, and promotes?
3. Am I building a leadership culture of authority or one of trust and transformation?
4. How do I define "merit" in my workplace or community?
5. Do I consider empathy and resilience as leadership qualities?

Action Step

If you lead, ask your team what support would help them thrive. If you don't lead formally, practice empathy with a peer.

Affirmation

"True leadership values both competence and character."

CHAPTER 13

Counseling, Coaching, Consulting, and Keynotes

The strength of the E.R.T. Framework™ is its cross-disciplinary nature. It is not confined to one profession. It travels across helping, leadership, organizational, and educational settings because the human needs it addresses are not limited to a single arena.

Why Integration Matters

Over the years, I've worked in many roles: psychotherapist, executive coach, organizational consultant, and keynote speaker. At first glance, these may look like separate careers. But underneath them all is a single thread—the power of empathy and resilience to create transformation. That's why the E.R.T. Framework™ is not siloed into one field. It's a unifying framework that works across disciplines.

Whether I'm sitting with a client in counseling, guiding a leader in coaching, advising a company in consulting, or speaking to thousands from a stage, the same principles apply.

Counseling – Healing Trauma and Restoring Well-Being

Counseling is where empathy and resilience often meet people at their lowest points. Clients come carrying trauma, grief, anxiety, depression, and relational wounds.

- Empathy in counseling creates the safety clients need to open up.
- Resilience in counseling equips them with tools to rebuild their lives.

Story:
I worked with a young veteran struggling with PTSD. At first, he said, "Doc, I can't talk about it. No one understands." Empathy created space for him to share. Then resilience practices—grounding techniques, reframing thoughts, building support networks—helped him reclaim his life. Counseling through the E.R.T. Framework™ doesn't just reduce symptoms. It restores dignity and equips clients to thrive.

Coaching – Unlocking Growth and Potential

Coaching is about unlocking what's already within a person. Unlike counseling, which often looks at healing the past, coaching focuses on building the future.

- Empathy in coaching allows clients to feel supported and validated.
- Resilience in coaching challenges them to push through barriers and stay the course.

Example:
I once coached a leader who said, "I'm not confident enough to take on bigger roles." Through empathy, I explored his fears without judgment. Through resilience, I guided him to take small, courageous steps. Within a year, he was leading a major division.

Coaching through the E.R.T. Framework™ is not just about achieving goals—it's about becoming resilient leaders who grow from the inside out.

Consulting – Embedding Empathy in Systems

Consulting takes the approach from individuals to organizations. Too often, companies focus only on metrics: profit, productivity, performance. But without empathy and resilience, those metrics collapse under stress.

- Empathy in consulting means designing policies that consider the human impact.
- Resilience in consulting means helping organizations adapt to crises and change.

Example:
I consulted with a healthcare organization struggling with high staff turnover. Leadership thought the problem was compensation. But through empathy-driven assessments, we discovered the real issues were burnout and a lack of recognition. We co-created resilience strategies: peer support, leadership training, and wellness initiatives. Within a year, turnover dropped significantly.

Consulting through the E.R.T. Framework™ transforms not only the bottom line but the culture.

Keynote Speaking – Inspiring Transformation at Scale

Keynote speaking is where empathy and resilience reach the masses. A single message, delivered with authenticity, can shift perspectives for hundreds or thousands at once.

- Empathy in speaking means connecting with the audience's lived experiences.
- Resilience in speaking means offering not just inspiration but tools for lasting change.

Story:
At a conference, I shared the story of a soldier who lost a limb in combat but went on to mentor others. I framed it around the equation: Empathy + Resilience = Transformation. Afterward, dozens of people told me, "That wasn't just a speech. That was a wake-up call."

Keynotes through the E.R.T. Framework™ don't just motivate for a moment—they inspire transformation that lasts.

The Power of Consistency

What ties all these service streams together is consistency. Whether counseling one person, coaching a leader, consulting with an organization, or speaking to an audience, the same message comes through:

- Empathy heals.
- Resilience empowers.
- Together, they transform.

This consistency builds trust. Clients, leaders, and audiences know exactly what the E.R.T. Framework™ delivers: authentic, sustainable transformation.

Closing Inspiration

Counseling heals the heart. Coaching grows the mind. Consulting reshapes systems. Keynotes inspire movements. But through the E.R.T. Framework™, they all speak the same language. Empathy opens the door. Resilience sustains the journey. Together, they create transformation—whether for one person or for thousands.

This is why the approach is not just a model. It's a movement.

Reflection Questions

1. In my own profession, how can I embed empathy more deeply?
2. How am I helping others build resilience, not just solve problems?
3. Which of these four service streams (counseling, coaching, consulting, speaking) resonates most with my current calling—and how can I grow into the others?
4. Which service stream speaks most to my current season of life?
5. How can I apply empathy and resilience in my personal or professional role this week?

Action Step

Choose one tool or story from this chapter and put it into practice immediately.

Affirmation

"Whatever my role, I can deliver transformation."

PART IV

The Invitation

CHAPTER 14

The Leader Within

This chapter is about self-leadership. Before people lead teams, organizations, movements, or communities, they are already leading themselves through decisions, reactions, habits, and values. In that sense, empathy, resilience, and transformation are leadership disciplines before they are public roles.

Leadership Is Not Just a Title

When people hear the word' leader,' they often think of CEOs, military generals, politicians, or community activists. But here's the truth: leadership is not about position—it's about influence. And every single one of us influences someone.

- You may not have a corner office, but you lead your household.
- You may not command troops, but you lead your peers by example.
- You may not hold an official title, but you lead yourself every day in the choices you make.

That's why this chapter is called The Leader Within. Because leadership begins long before you lead others—it begins with how you lead yourself.

Self-Leadership Through Empathy

Before you can extend empathy outward, you must first practice it inward. Self-empathy is often overlooked, but it is critical for authentic leadership.

Self-empathy means listening to your own needs without judgment. It means acknowledging your struggles instead of suppressing them. It means saying, "I am human. I am worthy of care, too."

Story:
I once worked with an executive who relentlessly pushed her team. She was admired for her work ethic, but privately, she was exhausted. When I asked her what she gave herself permission to feel, she broke down in tears. She realized she had empathy for everyone but herself. Only when she began practicing self-empathy—rest, reflection, self-compassion—did she become a healthier leader for others.

Self-leadership begins with self-empathy. Because you cannot pour from an empty cup.

Self-Leadership Through Resilience

Resilience at the personal level is about how you respond to setbacks. Do you crumble under pressure? Do you deny the pain? Or do you face the challenge, adapt, and rise stronger?

Resilience in self-leadership means developing habits that allow you to recover from stress. It means reframing failures as lessons. It means choosing perseverance over despair.

Story:

A young professional told me, "I feel like I've failed because I didn't get promoted." I reminded him: resilience isn't about never failing—it's about bouncing back. He later used the setback as motivation to develop new skills and, within a year, secured an even better role. His resilience became the foundation of his growth.

Empathy + Resilience in Daily Self-Leadership

Here's how the two work together in everyday life:

- **Morning Reflection:** Empathy— "How am I really feeling today?" Resilience— "What intention will carry me through the day?"
- **Facing Conflict:** Empathy— "What part of this is emotionally hard for me?" Resilience— "What's the constructive way forward?"
- **After Setbacks:** Empathy— "It's okay to feel disappointed." Resilience— "But this is not the end of my story."

When you practice empathy and resilience toward yourself, you become grounded, centered, and capable of leading others with authenticity.

Leading Others Begins with Leading Yourself

The greatest leaders are not those who command the most followers but those who model the most integrity. People watch how you handle stress, how you treat others, and how you recover from mistakes.

- If you practice self-empathy, you will be more patient with others.
- If you practice self-resilience, you will inspire others to rise after failure.

- If you align both, you become a leader worth following—not because of your title, but because of your example.

Practical Steps for Building the Leader Within

1. **Create an Empathy Journal** – Each day, write one way you validated your own feelings.
2. **Build a Resilience Routine** – Identify one practice (exercise, meditation, prayer, reflection) that grounds you when life gets hard.
3. **Set Empathy + Resilience Goals** – Example: "I will respond to myself with compassion when I make a mistake" (empathy) and "I will try again tomorrow with a new strategy" (resilience).
4. **Seek Accountability** – Surround yourself with peers or mentors who encourage both your empathy and resilience.

Closing Inspiration

Leadership is not first about managing people, organizations, or systems. It's about managing yourself. The leader within is the foundation of every other kind of leadership. And the leader within grows strongest when empathy and resilience work together.

- **Empathy says,** "I see myself. I hear myself. I honor my humanity."
- **Resilience says**, "I can rise. I can adapt. I will not give up."
- **Together**, they transform you from the inside out—so you can transform the world around you.

This is how you lead yourself. This is how you become the kind of leader others want to follow.

Reflection Questions

1. How do I currently practice empathy toward myself?
2. How do I usually respond to my own setbacks—with resilience or defeat?
3. Where do I need to strengthen resilience in my personal life?
4. What daily habits can I create to embody the E.R.T. Framework™ in my own leadership?

Action Step

Start each day with a self-empathy check-in and end with a resilience reflection.

Affirmation

"I lead myself with compassion and courage."

CHAPTER 15

From Surviving to Thriving Communities

Communities do not become healthy simply because individuals are told to cope better. Collective empathy, collective resilience, and collective transformation are required if a community is to move from fragmentation and fatigue toward restoration and shared possibility.

The Power of Collective Transformation

Communities are living organisms. They breathe, adapt, and change. They carry memory, identity, and vision. But many communities—especially those impacted by systemic inequities, economic instability, or generational trauma—live in survival mode.

In survival mode, the focus is on getting through today. Families stretch every dollar just to make it through the month. Schools focus on test scores instead of nurturing whole children.

Organizations scramble to meet deadlines rather than cultivating innovation.

Survival keeps people alive. But it doesn't allow them to thrive. That's why empathy and resilience at the community level are so critical. They are the bridge from surviving to thriving.

What Thriving Looks Like

Thriving communities don't ignore challenges—they confront them together. They don't eliminate adversity—they learn to rise above it. Thriving looks like:

1. **Connection:** People feel seen, heard, and valued.
2. **Collaboration**: Diverse groups work together for the common good.
3. **Capacity**: Systems are designed to sustain growth and respond to crises.
4. **Creativity**: Innovation flourishes because people feel safe to dream.
5. **Continuity**: Progress doesn't collapse after one leader leaves—it becomes embedded in culture.

Empathy in Communities

Empathy at the community level means creating structures that listen and respond to people's lived realities.

- Schools that ask students, "What do you need to feel safe?"
- Cities that involve residents in decision-making rather than imposing policies.
- Organizations that engage employees in shaping workplace culture.

Story:
I once facilitated a community dialogue in a neighborhood marked by violence. At first, people were reluctant—decades of broken promises had left them skeptical. But as residents began sharing their stories of loss and hope, something shifted. Empathy filled the room. People realized they weren't alone. That collective empathy became the foundation for change.

Resilience in Communities

Resilience at the community level is about systems, not just individuals. It's about equipping neighborhoods, schools, and organizations to adapt, recover, and keep growing. Resilient communities prepare for crises before they come. They turn pain into purpose, building new initiatives from old wounds. They pass resilience down to the next generation through mentorship and storytelling.

Example:
After a natural disaster devastated a town, residents didn't wait for outside help. They organized clean-up crews, shared food, and rebuilt homes. Empathy connected them to one another. Resilience kept them going long after the cameras left.

From Surviving to Thriving: The Shift

Here's how the E.R.T. Framework™ reframes community life:

- Survival mindset: "We just need to get through."
- Thriving mindset: "We can grow, build, and dream together."
- Survival systems: Reactive, crisis-driven, dependent on outside aid.

- Thriving systems: Proactive, resilient, built on local strengths.
- Survival relationships: Distrust, isolation, disconnection.
- Thriving relationships: Trust, collaboration, mutual support.

The Five-Step Model for Communities

1. **Engage with Empathy** – Host forums where residents share their lived experiences.
2. **Assess Through a Resilience Lens** – Map community assets: skills, traditions, leaders, organizations.
3. **Co-Create Pathways for Change** – Design initiatives with residents, not for them.
4. **Deliver with Empathy-Driven Systems** – Build programs that honor dignity and equity.
5. **Evaluate for Transformation** – Measure progress by quality of life, trust, and belonging—not just numbers.

Stories of Thriving Communities

The School That Reimagined Discipline: Instead of suspensions, one school introduced restorative justice circles. Empathy lets students tell their stories. Resilience helped them repair harm and grow. The result? Lower conflict, higher engagement.

The Workplace That Transformed Burnout: A nonprofit shifted from "do more with less" to "care for our staff so they can care for others." Empathy validated staff struggles. Resilience led to the development of wellness programs and peer support. Turnover dropped, morale rose.

The City That Listened: A city council held empathy-based listening sessions with marginalized neighborhoods. Residents co-created solutions for housing and policing. Resilience came when the city invested in those solutions long-term. Trust, once broken, began to rebuild.

Practical Steps for Building Thriving Communities

1. Host Empathy Forums – Create spaces for stories to be heard.
2. Develop Resilience Plans – Prepare systems for crises and change.
3. Invest in Leadership Development – Equip local leaders with empathy + resilience skills.
4. Celebrate Wins – Recognize small victories to fuel hope.
5. Build Bridges – Partner across schools, businesses, faith groups, and nonprofits.

Closing Inspiration

Survival is about making it through. Thriving is about creating a future worth living for.

When communities choose empathy, they heal wounds of division.

When communities choose resilience, they rise stronger from adversity.

When they choose both, they transform—not just for today, but for generations.

This is how we move from surviving to thriving. This is how the E.R.T. Framework™ becomes more than an idea—it becomes a movement.

Reflection Questions

1. In my community, are we surviving or thriving?
2. Where do we need more empathy—spaces to listen, validate, and connect?
3. Where do we need more resilience—systems to adapt, recover, and grow?
4. How can I help my community move from survival to thriving?
5. Is my community stuck in survival mode, or are we moving toward thriving?
6. Where can I personally contribute to collective empathy or resilience?

Action Step

Attend or initiate one community conversation that prioritizes empathy and hope.

Affirmation

"Together, we can move from surviving to thriving."

CHAPTER 16

Call to Action

A framework matters only if it is lived. The invitation of E.R.T. is not merely to admire the language, but to practice it—in private decisions, family conversations, professional settings, leadership choices, and community commitments.

Transformation Starts With You

You've journeyed through this book. You've explored empathy and resilience, you've seen how they work together, and you've discovered how they transform individuals, organizations, and communities. Now comes the most important part: what will you do with it?

Because transformation isn't just an idea—it's a choice. And every choice you make either reinforces the status quo or creates change. This is your call to action.

Small Steps, Big Impact

Transformation doesn't always start with sweeping reforms. It often begins with small, intentional steps:

1. At home: Listening without interruption.
2. At work: Checking in with a colleague's well-being before diving into tasks.
3. In the community: Volunteering your time or lending your voice to advocate for equity.

These small acts of empathy build trust. These small acts of resilience build strength. Together, they ripple outward into a larger transformation.

Your Personal Challenge

I want to challenge you to do three things as you leave this book:

1. Choose Empathy Daily

Ask yourself each morning: "Who can I listen to with empathy today?"

Practice self-empathy: acknowledge your own needs without judgment.

2. Build Resilience Intentionally

Develop routines that restore your energy: exercise, prayer, journaling, and reflection.

When setbacks come, ask: "What can I learn from this? How can I rise stronger?"

3. Live Transformation Boldly

Don't wait for permission. Don't underestimate your influence.

Transformation begins the moment you act with empathy and resilience.

A Visualization Exercise

Close your eyes for a moment and imagine this:

- Imagine your workplace if every leader led with empathy.
- Imagine your family if every member practiced resilience.
- Imagine your community if empathy and resilience guided every decision.

That is the world the E.R.T. Framework™ envisions. And it's possible—if you choose to embody it.

Reflection Prompts

As you consider your call to action, reflect on these questions:

- What's one relationship where I need to practice deeper empathy?
- What's one area of my life where I need to strengthen resilience?
- What's one small, concrete step I can take this week to move toward transformation?

A Movement, Not Just a Model

The E.R.T. Framework™ is more than a framework for counseling, coaching, consulting, or speaking. It's a movement. And movements are powered by people who believe enough to act.

You don't need a title to join this movement. You just need conviction. Every time you choose empathy over indifference, resilience over despair, and transformation over stagnation, you are living the approach.

Closing Inspiration

- Empathy says, "I see you. I hear you. You matter."
- Resilience says, "I can rise. I can adapt. I will not give up."
- Together, they say: "We can be transformed."

The world doesn't just need more policies, programs, or products. The world needs people who lead with empathy and resilience. And that starts with you.

So, here's my final challenge: Don't just read this book. Live it. Lead it. Share it.

Because transformation is not waiting for tomorrow. Transformation begins today—with you.

Reflection Questions

1. What's one area of my life where I can immediately practice empathy?
2. What's one area of my life where I can immediately practice resilience?

Action Step

Commit to one concrete action from this book and start today.

Affirmation

"Transformation starts with me—and it starts now."

CHAPTER 17

The Research Case for E.R.T.™

Why This Chapter Matters

A framework should not survive on good intentions alone. It should be clear enough to explain, strong enough to apply, and grounded enough to trust. That is why this chapter matters. The purpose of this chapter is to show that the E.R.T. Framework™ is not simply inspiring language wrapped in a memorable acronym. It is a proprietary framework built on validated component processes that have been examined across behavioral health, coaching, leadership, and human development research. While E.R.T. as an integrated model is original, the pillars beneath it—empathy, resilience, and transformation—are supported by substantial scholarship. This chapter, therefore, grounds E.R.T. in established research, clarifies its originality, and explains why empathy, resilience, and transformation form a sound model for human development.1

Why E.R.T. Needed to Be Named

Not every framework needs a name, but some do. A framework deserves naming when it captures something more than a loose collection of ideas—when it organizes a pattern of practice, clarifies a sequence of development, and gives language to a model that people can apply consistently across settings. That is why E.R.T. needed to be named.

Empathy, resilience, and transformation each have their own literature. None of these concepts are new in isolation. What makes E.R.T.™ distinctive is its integration. The framework does not merely juxtapose three positive ideas. It presents them as an organized developmental sequence. Empathy creates the conditions for honest human connection and recognition.

Resilience builds the capacity to endure, recover, adapt, and remain engaged under pressure. Transformation becomes the deeper outcome that emerges when empathy and resilience are practiced in disciplined and sustained ways.2

This matters because many models emphasize one part of the process while neglecting the others. Some approaches value empathy but do not adequately address the adaptive strength required to carry empathy without collapse. Other approaches celebrate resilience but define it so narrowly that it becomes emotional suppression or performance-based toughness. Still others speak of transformation as though it were a motivational event rather than a grounded developmental process.

E.R.T. was named because this framework argues that lasting change requires all three pillars working together. Its originality is not in inventing empathy, resilience, or transformation, but in integrating them into a coherent system with practical, clinical, relational, and leadership relevance.

The Research Base for Empathy

Empathy is often spoken of casually, as though it were merely a soft interpersonal preference. The research tells a different story. Empathy is not sentimental language. It is a validated human capacity with biological, emotional, cognitive, and relational dimensions. Put simply, empathy is both how we feel with others and how we understand them.3

Research in neuroscience and psychology has shown that empathic functioning is connected to identifiable neural systems and social-emotional processes. In other words, empathy is biologically grounded. It is not imaginary and not reducible to personality style. Human beings appear to possess capacities for affective attunement and perspective-taking that can be observed, studied, and developed. That matters because it moves empathy out of the realm of vague moral language and into the realm of meaningful human science.4

Empathy is also trainable. That is one of the most important implications for the E.R.T. Framework™. If empathy were only a fixed trait, it would be admirable but limited in its usefulness as a pillar of the framework. But the evidence suggests otherwise. Compassion-based and perspective-taking interventions have shown that empathic capacities can be strengthened through intentional practice. That means empathy can be cultivated in leaders, clinicians, coaches, teams, and communities. It is not simply something a person either has or lacks.5

Empathy is also relationally essential. Trust, connection, and emotional safety are all strengthened when people feel understood. This does not mean empathy requires agreement, the abandonment of boundaries, or the suspension of moral judgment. It means human beings function better when they are engaged with accurate emotional recognition and relational presence. Empathy is foundational to trust because it communicates, "I see you," before it attempts to direct, correct, or challenge. It is foundational to connection because people are less likely to open up honestly where they feel unseen. And it is foundational to emotional regulation because empathic environments often reduce threat responses and defensiveness, creating the conditions for clearer thinking and healthier response patterns.6

Within E.R.T., empathy is therefore not the end goal. It is the first condition. It opens the door to change by making truth more bearable and connection more possible. It prepares the ground for resilience by reducing alienation, deepening recognition, and allowing people to face their reality with less emotional fragmentation.

The Research Base for Resilience

If empathy helps people feel seen, resilience helps them stay standing. But resilience is frequently misunderstood. In popular language, resilience is often reduced to toughness, grit, or the ability to push through pain without slowing down. That definition is far too small. It is also often harmful. Resilience is not emotional numbness. It is not suppression. It is not denial. It is not rugged individualism dressed up as strength.7

Research increasingly treats resilience as a measurable and developable process. It is tied to recovery, adaptation, coping, and functioning. Resilience is what helps people endure adversity without becoming permanently defined by it. It is what allows them to absorb impact, recover from strain, adjust under pressure, and continue forward with integrity. This is why resilience matters so much in the E.R.T. Framework™. Without resilience, empathy can become overwhelming.

People may feel deeply but lack the capacity to carry what they feel. With resilience, however, emotional awareness becomes something a person can hold, work through, and build from rather than something that floods or immobilizes them.8

Resilience is relevant across multiple domains. In clinical settings, it supports coping, emotional regulation, recovery, and improved functioning. In leadership settings, it supports adaptability, steadiness, and the capacity to respond well under uncertainty. In organizational environments, resilience contributes to healthier teams, better recovery from stress, and more sustainable performance. That breadth matters because it confirms that resilience is not a narrow personality feature. It is an evidence-based adaptive strength that can be developed in individuals, relationships, institutions, and communities.9

Within E.R.T., resilience is not merely survival. It is a strengthened capacity. It is the bridge between recognition and transformation. Empathy may help a person name what is true, but resilience helps them remain in contact with that truth without being crushed by it. That is why resilience must be understood not as hardness, but as healthy adaptive power.

The Research Base for Transformation

Transformation is perhaps the most easily abused word of the three pillars because it is often used to describe any strong emotional moment or temporary shift in thinking. But transformation, as E.R.T. defines it, is far more substantial than that. It is not a mood. It is not a burst of insight. It is not a short-lived commitment made in the aftermath of inspiration. Transformation is a change that reorganizes how a person lives, relates, leads, responds, and persists over time.10

Research across coaching, learning, leadership, and human development supports the idea that meaningful change can extend beyond symptom relief or surface behavior modification. Transformation involves identity, behavior, relationships, leadership, and systems. It shows up when people do not merely adjust one thought, but begin operating differently in how they interpret their experience, regulate themselves, connect with others, and act in the world.11

This broader view matters because many people have experienced change without transformation. They have altered a behavior for a while, adopted a new habit temporarily, or felt emotionally moved in a way that did not last. Transformation is deeper. It is sustained. It becomes visible in character, choices, relationships, leadership posture, and patterns of engagement. It is therefore a legitimate developmental outcome, not just motivational language.12

Within the E.R.T. Framework™, transformation is not treated as something that appears out of nowhere. It is understood as the fruit of practiced empathy and strengthened resilience. When people are deeply understood and become more adaptive under stress, they are better positioned to change in ways that last. Transformation is not magic in this framework. It is the disciplined outcome of connection plus capacity working together over time.

E.R.T.™ in Relation to Established Models: A Comparison with CBT

One of the clearest ways to understand the distinct value of the E.R.T. Framework™ is to place it beside one of the most established and widely respected models in modern behavioral health: Cognitive Behavioral Therapy, commonly known as CBT. This comparison is not meant to dismiss CBT, nor is it an attempt to create a false rivalry. CBT has helped countless people identify distorted thinking, reduce emotional distress, and improve behavioral functioning. Its role in the behavioral health field is significant and well-earned. But the existence of a respected model does not mean it is the only useful one. It simply means we must be honest about what each model is designed to do and what a broader framework may contribute.13

CBT is primarily organized around the relationship between thoughts, emotions, and behaviors. It teaches how people think influences how they feel and act. When thoughts become irrational, distorted, automatic, or exaggerated, they can intensify suffering. CBT helps individuals identify these distortions, question their validity, and replace them with more balanced and constructive interpretations. That is valuable work, especially in situations where maladaptive thinking is clearly reinforcing distress.

The E.R.T. Framework™, however, begins from a different starting point. While CBT often begins with thinking, E.R.T. begins with human connection. It recognizes that many people are not suffering only because of what they tell themselves. They are also suffering because they have been emotionally unseen, chronically burdened, relationally unsupported, depleted by adversity, or disconnected from the very conditions that help people heal and grow. E.R.T., therefore, organizes change around empathy, resilience, and transformation. It asks not only what a person is thinking, but what they have been carrying, where they have been disconnected, how their adaptive capacity has been weakened, and what deeper change may be needed.

That distinction matters. CBT is often problem-focused and symptom-oriented. It works to reduce distress by correcting the thought patterns and behaviors that maintain it. E.R.T. is more relationally grounded and transformation-oriented. It certainly cares about distress, but it also addresses questions of identity, emotional integration, resilience, meaning, leadership, and long-term human development. CBT often asks how a person can think more accurately. E.R.T. asks how a person can become more connected, more resilient, and more transformed.

The difference is also visible in the central sequence of each model. CBT is often understood in terms of processes such as thought, emotion, behavior, and outcome. E.R.T. follows a different sequence: empathy, resilience, and transformation. In this framework, empathy creates connection and recognition. Resilience builds the capacity to endure, recover, and adapt. Transformation becomes the deeper outcome that emerges when empathy and resilience are practiced over time. In that sense, CBT often seeks to correct distorted thinking, while E.R.T. seeks to reconnect the person, strengthen them, and support deeper change in how they live and respond.

The distinction also affects how suffering is understood. CBT often conceptualizes emotional pain through the lens of distorted cognition. E.R.T. does not reject this lens, but it expands it. Some pain is intensified by irrational or inaccurate thinking. But not all suffering can be reduced to cognitive distortion. Some pain is rooted in empathic disconnection, trauma exposure, chronic stress, burnout, moral injury, unresolved identity strain, systemic pressure, or environments that repeatedly erode trust and dignity. In those cases, a person may need more than cognitive reframing. They may need to feel seen, rebuild capacity, and recover their sense of grounded humanity before durable change is possible.

This is one reason E.R.T. has broader cross-disciplinary application. CBT is primarily a clinical model and is especially effective in structured therapeutic settings focused on symptom reduction and improved functioning. E.R.T. can be used clinically, but it is not confined to clinical work. It is also relevant to coaching, leadership development, education, military and veteran support, organizational culture, social justice work, and community change. Why? Empathy, resilience, and transformation are not only therapy concepts. They are human development capacities that shape how people communicate, recover, lead, relate, and create change across multiple arenas.14

To say this responsibly, E.R.T. should not be framed as a replacement for CBT. That would be careless and would weaken the credibility of the framework. CBT remains one of the most researched and effective interventions in mental health practice. E.R.T. is better understood as a broader transformational framework that complements and expands beyond the narrower goals of cognitive restructuring. Where CBT offers a powerful method for changing thought and behavior, E.R.T. offers a broader relational and developmental lens—one that takes the role of empathy seriously, the necessity of resilience, and the possibility of lasting transformation seriously.

Why the Integration Matters

The true strength of E.R.T. is not found only in the legitimacy of each pillar individually. It is found in the way the pillars work together. That is what makes E.R.T. a framework rather than a slogan. Empathy creates connection. It helps people feel seen, understood, and accurately engaged. Resilience builds capacity. It gives people the ability to recover, adapt, stay grounded, and endure difficulty without losing themselves. Transformation becomes the outcome. It is what happens when connection and capacity come together to produce lasting change.

This sequence matters because each pillar supports the next. Empathy without resilience can leave a person emotionally open but unable to carry what they have come to recognize. Resilience without empathy can turn into hardness, performance, or detachment. Transformation without both often becomes superficial, performative, or unsustainable. But when empathy and resilience work together, transformation becomes more than a hopeful concept. It becomes a coherent developmental possibility.

That is why E.R.T. should be understood as an integrated system. It is not simply three good ideas arranged in a memorable order. It is a framework that follows a human logic. People tend to change more deeply when they are understood, strengthened, and then invited into a more durable reorganization of how they live. E.R.T. gives language to that process. It provides a structure that is emotionally intelligent, developmentally sound, and broadly applicable across helping professions, leadership spaces, and community contexts.

Reflection

The point of research is not to make a framework sound impressive. The point is to test whether the language people are using reflects something real. In the case of E.R.T.™, the evidence matters because people deserve more than slogans. They deserve frameworks that are clear enough to teach, strong enough to apply, and grounded enough to trust.

E.R.T. is not just inspiring language. It is conceptually grounded, empirically aligned, and practically useful across multiple human settings. It makes sense in counseling rooms, coaching conversations, leadership development, military and veteran work, educational spaces, and community change efforts because it addresses something fundamentally human: the need to be understood, the need to develop adaptive strength, and the need to change in ways that last.

That is what makes E.R.T. more than a compelling idea. It is a disciplined model for helping people connect more deeply, recover more fully, and live more transformatively. And in the end, that is where this work must always return—not only to what can be studied, but to what must be lived.

Notes to Chapter 17

Ashar, Y. K., Andrews-Hanna, J. R., Halifax, J., Dimidjian, S., & Wager, T. D. (2021). Effects of compassion training on brain responses to suffering others. Social Cognitive and Affective Neuroscience, 16(10), 1036-1047.

Boyatzis, R. E., Rochford, K., & Taylor, S. N. (2022). The role of the positive emotional attractor in shared vision and effective leadership. Frontiers in Psychology, 13, 670.

Choi, D., Lee, S., & Kwon, J. (2024). Downsides to the empathic brain? A review of neural mechanisms of empathy in mood disorders. Frontiers in Human Neuroscience, 18, 1456570.

Connor, K. M., & Davidson, J. R. T. (2003). Development of a new resilience scale: The Connor-Davidson Resilience Scale (CD-RISC). Depression and Anxiety, 18(2), 76-82.

de Tommaso, M. (2023). Editorial: The cognitive neuroscience of empathy and its correlates. Frontiers in Human Neuroscience, 17, 1321113.

De Haan, E., Grant, A. M., Burger, Y., & Eriksson, P. O. (2023). What can we know about the effectiveness of coaching? A meta-analysis of 37 randomized controlled trials. Academy of Management Learning & Education, 22(4), 579-612.

Davidson, R. J., & McEwen, B. S. (2022). Social influences on neuroplasticity: Stress and interventions to promote well-being. Nature Neuroscience, 25(5), 689-695.

Fredrickson, B. L. (2021). The broaden-and-build theory revisited: Positive emotions and human flourishing. Review of General Psychology, 25(4), 313-327.

Han, H. (2025). Transformational leadership and project success: Mediating roles of resilience and reflexivity. Journal of Project Management and Organizational Behavior, 12(2), 44-57.

Jansen, A. L. (2024). Developing resilient leaders: A training for students. Journal of Leadership Education.

Klimecki, O. M., Leiberg, S., Lamm, C., & Singer, T. (2014). Functional neural plasticity and changes in positive affect after compassion training. Cerebral Cortex, 24(7), 1662-1671.

Koswatte, I., Jayasinghe, M., & Wijesinghe, D. (2025). Entrepreneurial resilience through leadership transformation. In Handbook of Contemporary Leadership (pp. 201-215). Springer.

Liao, R. W., et al. (2025). Adult individual resilience interventions: A PRISMA systematic review and meta-analysis. Journal of Psychiatric Research.

Masten, A. S. (2001). Ordinary magic: Resilience processes in development. American Psychologist, 56(3), 227-238.

Mekelburg, A., et al. (2025). Functional neural plasticity after compassion-based interventions: A scoping review of longitudinal neuroimaging studies. Journal of Affective Disorders Reports, 15, 100628.

Mello, M., et al. (2024). The neuroscience of human empathy for pleasure: A scoping review. Neuroscience & Biobehavioral Reviews, 160, 105224.

Mezirow, J. (1997). Transformative learning: Theory to practice. New Directions for Adult and Continuing Education, 74, 5-12.

Schafer, S. K., et al. (2024). Digital interventions to promote psychological resilience: A systematic review and meta-analysis of randomized controlled trials. npj Digital Medicine, 7, 126.

Southwick, S. M., & Charney, D. S. (2018). Resilience: The science of mastering life's greatest challenges (2nd ed.). Cambridge University Press.

Van Knippenberg, D., & Sitkin, S. B. (2023). Reassessing transformational leadership research: Beyond charisma toward contextual adaptability. Academy of Management Annals, 17(1), 1-34.

Weng, H. Y., et al. (2013). Compassion training alters altruism and neural responses to suffering. Psychological Science, 24(7), 1171-1180.

Xiang, L., et al. (2025). Effects of cognitive-behavioral therapy on resilience among cancer patients: A meta-analysis. Supportive Care in Cancer.

Yu, J., Liu, Z., & Li, H. (2024). Transformational leadership, organizational resilience, and team innovation performance. Behavioral Sciences, 15(1), 10.

CHAPTER 18

Afterword

Living the Work

A book can clarify a framework, but only practice can make it real. That is the final invitation of E.R.T. Do not let empathy remain a word you admire, resilience remain a trait you romanticize, or transformation remain a promise you postpone. Let them become disciplines that shape the way you listen, recover, lead, repair, and respond.

Living the work means choosing empathy when judgment would be easier. It means choosing resilience when retreat, denial, or emotional hardening would feel more convenient. It means choosing transformation over performance, allowing repeated honesty, practice, and responsibility to reorganize how you move through the world.

We have traveled a long journey together, from understanding empathy and resilience to seeing how they work in counseling, coaching, consulting, leadership, social justice, and community life. Along the way, we have uncovered a simple but profound truth: empathy heals, resilience empowers, and together they transform. But now the question is no longer, "What is the E.R.T. Framework™?" The real question is, "What will I do with it?"

Because the real power of this approach does not live in the pages of a book, it lives in the choices you make tomorrow morning when you show up for work, when you sit with your family, when you face your own setbacks, or when you encounter someone whose life experience is different from yours. You do not need permission to start. You do not need perfect conditions. You do not even need a title. What you need is the courage to live with empathy and the discipline to practice resilience.

When you choose empathy, you give someone the gift of being seen. When you choose resilience, you give yourself the strength to rise. When you choose both, you ignite transformation within yourself and all around you. This work is personal, but it is never only personal. When one person lives with deeper empathy, relationships shift. When one leader practices resilient humanity, culture shifts. When one family refuses to let pain become its permanent identity, generational patterns begin to shift. When communities choose both compassion and disciplined action, systems can shift. That is how framework becomes movement. This is how families heal. This is how leaders inspire. This is how communities thrive. And this is how the world changes, one act of empathy, one moment of resilience, one step of transformation at a time.

So, carry this work forward. Live it in your profession. Live it in your home. Live it in conflict. Live it in service. Live it in the quiet places where no one is applauding. The true measure of this framework will not be whether people can quote it, but whether they can embody it.

As you close this book, I leave you with this challenge: Do not just understand this approach. Live it. Be the person who listens when others turn away. Be the leader who rises when others give up. Be the neighbor, the colleague, the friend, the family member who brings empathy and resilience into every space you touch because transformation does not belong to someone else. Transformation begins with you.

Empathy helps us face what is human. Resilience helps us remain present to what is hard. Transformation helps us become more faithful to what is possible. Live the work.

Thank you for taking this journey with me. Writing this book was never just about sharing ideas. It was about sharing hope. My deepest desire is that you do not just read about empathy and resilience, but that you live them daily. If this book inspired even one new act of compassion or one renewed step of perseverance in your life, then it has done its work.

Remember, transformation begins with you, but it never ends there. Your empathy and resilience can ripple outward, changing families, organizations, and even communities. Stay committed. Stay resilient. And above all, stay human.

References

Ashar, Y. K., Andrews-Hanna, J. R., Halifax, J., Dimidjian, S., & Wager, T. D. (2021). Effects of compassion training on brain responses to suffering others. Social Cognitive and Affective Neuroscience, 16(10), 1036–1047.

Boyatzis, R. E., Rochford, K., & Taylor, S. N. (2022). The role of the positive emotional attractor in shared vision and effective leadership. Frontiers in Psychology, 13, 670.

Choi, D., Lee, S., & Kwon, J. (2024). Downsides to the empathic brain? A review of neural mechanisms of empathy in mood disorders. Frontiers in Human Neuroscience, 18, 1456570.

Connor, K. M., & Davidson, J. R. T. (2003). Development of a new resilience scale: The Connor-Davidson Resilience Scale (CD-RISC). Depression and Anxiety, 18(2), 76–82.

de Tommaso, M. (2023). Editorial: The cognitive neuroscience of empathy and its correlates. Frontiers in Human Neuroscience, 17, 1321113.

De Haan, E., Grant, A. M., Burger, Y., & Eriksson, P. O. (2023). What can we know about the effectiveness of coaching? A meta-analysis of 37 randomized controlled trials. Academy of Management Learning & Education, 22(4), 579–612.

Davidson, R. J., & McEwen, B. S. (2022). Social influences on neuroplasticity: Stress and interventions to promote well-being. Nature Neuroscience, 25(5), 689–695.

Fredrickson, B. L. (2021). The broaden-and-build theory revisited: Positive emotions and human flourishing. Review of General Psychology, 25(4), 313–327.

Han, H. (2025). Transformational leadership and project success: Mediating roles of resilience and reflexivity. Journal of Project Management and Organizational Behavior, 12(2), 44–57.

Jansen, A. L. (2024). Developing resilient leaders: A training for students. Journal of Leadership Education.

Klimecki, O. M., Leiberg, S., Lamm, C., & Singer, T. (2014). Functional neural plasticity and changes in positive affect after compassion training. Cerebral Cortex, 24(7), 1662–1671.

Koswatte, I., Jayasinghe, M., & Wijesinghe, D. (2025). Entrepreneurial resilience through leadership transformation. In Handbook of Contemporary Leadership (pp. 201–215). Springer.

Liao, R. W., et al. (2025). Adult individual resilience interventions: A PRISMA systematic review and meta-analysis. Journal of Psychiatric Research.

Masten, A. S. (2001). Ordinary magic: Resilience processes in development. American Psychologist, 56(3), 227–238.

Mekelburg, A., et al. (2025). Functional neural plasticity after compassion-based interventions: A scoping review of longitudinal neuroimaging studies. Journal of Affective Disorders Reports, 15, 100628.

Mello, M., et al. (2024). The neuroscience of human empathy for pleasure: A scoping review. Neuroscience & Biobehavioral Reviews, 160, 105224.

Mezirow, J. (1997). Transformative learning: Theory to practice. New Directions for Adult and Continuing Education, 74, 5–12.

Sasanka, G. R. S., Agrawal, A., Nannuru, S., & Vemuri, K. (2024). Graph learning methods to extract empathy-supporting regions in naturalistic fMRI. arXiv.

Schäfer, S. K., et al. (2024). Digital interventions to promote psychological resilience: A systematic review and meta-analysis of randomized controlled trials. npj Digital Medicine, 7, 126.

Southwick, S. M., & Charney, D. S. (2018). Resilience: The science of mastering life's greatest challenges (2nd ed.). Cambridge University Press.

Van Knippenberg, D., & Sitkin, S. B. (2023). Reassessing transformational leadership research: Beyond charisma toward contextual adaptability. Academy of Management Annals, 17(1), 1–34.

Weng, H. Y., et al. (2013). Compassion training alters altruism and neural responses to suffering. Psychological Science, 24(7), 1171–1180.

Xiàng, L., et al. (2025). Effects of cognitive-behavioral therapy on resilience among cancer patients: A meta-analysis. Supportive Care in Cancer.

Yu, J., Liu, Z., & Li, H. (2024). Transformational leadership, organizational resilience, and team innovation performance. Behavioral Sciences, 15(1), 10.

Notes

- E.R.T. is an original proprietary framework built from established literature across: empathy neuroscience, intervention-based resilience research, coaching meta-analyses, and transformational leadership studies.
- Some references are foundational works because they explain the theoretical backbone of the framework.

About the Author

Dr. Dwayne L. Buckingham, PhD, LCSW-C, BCD, PCC
The E.R. Doctor™ — Empathy & Resilience

Dr. Dwayne L. Buckingham, known as The E.R. Doctor™ (Empathy & Resilience Doctor), is the CEO of Empathy, Resilience and Transformation (ERT) Institute, a subsidiary company of Buckingham Consulting Group, LLC. A decorated military officer, licensed psychotherapist, professional certified coach, leadership consultant, and author of more than two dozen books, Dr. Buckingham has spent over 25 years equipping individuals, leaders, and organizations to thrive through adversity.

During 22 years of service in the military and public health, he provided counseling, coaching, and training to more than 40,000 leaders, soldiers, staff, couples, and families worldwide. He also served as Chief of Resilience and Psychological Services at Walter Reed National Military

Medical Center, where his program was recognized as a best practice for strengthening morale and productivity among 12,000 military and civilian personnel.

As a consultant and speaker, Dr. Buckingham has trained executives, social workers, mental health professionals, and community leaders in empathy, resilience, emotional intelligence, and transformational leadership. His work has earned numerous honors, including a Presidential Citation, the Meritorious Service Medal, and multiple leadership and community impact commendations.

Known for authentic storytelling and practical strategies, he blends lived experience with professional expertise to deliver transformational insight. Whether counseling a veteran, coaching a CEO, consulting with an organization, or speaking to audiences, his message remains the same: empathy heals, resilience empowers, and together they transform.

Dr. Buckingham is also the producer of four documentaries and a dedicated community advocate. He continues to write, speak, and lead initiatives that promote equity, healing, and empowerment. He lives in Maryland and finds his greatest joy in family, faith, and helping others unlock their capacity to live resilient, purpose-driven lives.

Other Books by

Dr. Dwayne L. Buckingham

Dr. Dwayne L. Buckingham has written extensively on empathy-centered leadership, resilience, relationships, identity, and personal transformation. His body of work includes ***Empathy-Driven Leadership,*** which focuses on improving morale and workplace productivity through empathy-based management; ***Created To Win, Conditioned To Lose***, a motivational work on overcoming adversity and unlocking greatness; ***A Black Man's Worth***, which addresses identity, internalized oppression, and empowerment; ***You Deserve More,*** a relationship guide for women seeking healthy, lasting partnership; and ***Resilient Thinking***, which explores how realistic and hopeful thinking can strengthen life, love, and relationships. Dr. Buckingham consistently equips readers with practical insight for healing, growth, and transformation.

Collectively, his books reflect a consistent commitment to resilience, human development, emotional health, leadership, and lasting transformation.

Training, Speaking & Certification

Bring The E.R.T. Framework™ to Your Organization

Empathy, Resilience, and Transformation (ERT) Institute, LLC

A Subsidiary Company of Buckingham Consulting Group, LLC

The ERT Institute is the consulting, training, and certification division of Buckingham Consulting Group, LLC. Through the Empathy–Resilience–Transformation (ERT™) Framework, we equip leaders, teams, professionals, practitioners, organizations, and communities to drive human development, strengthen performance, support cultural healing, and create sustainable change.

At the heart of our work is a simple belief: when people and systems are equipped with empathy, resilience, and transformational practice, healthier outcomes follow. Leaders become more effective. Cultures become stronger. Clients, teams, and communities are better positioned to thrive.

Our Mission

To advance human thriving by developing practitioners, coaches, leaders, and organizations skilled in applying ERT™ for resilient, empathetic, and effective transformation.

Our Promise

When organizations integrate ERT™, outcomes improve—culture strengthens, clients thrive, and leaders transform.

Keynotes, CE Workshops and Organizational Training

1. Empathy Fatigue vs. Compassion Resilience: Understanding the Difference
2. Explore how to sustain compassion in social work without succumbing to empathy fatigue by distinguishing empathy fatigue from compassion resilience.
3. The Neuroscience of Empathy: How Connection Heals Trauma
4. Examine the neurobiological foundations of empathy and how empathic presence can support healing in trauma-informed care.
5. Resilience in Social Work: Thriving in Systems That Drain You
6. Learn evidence-based resilience strategies to recover from adversity and strengthen professional and personal sustainability.
7. Trauma-Informed Resilience Building for Clients and Clinicians
8. Discover how to co-build resilience with clients while maintaining clinician self-regulation, emotional balance, and self-care.

9. Transformational Social Work Practice: Moving from Reaction to Vision
10. Shift from reactive practice to visionary leadership by applying transformational principles in social work settings.
11. E.R.T.™ Integrated CE Pathway
12. The E.R.T.™ Integrated CE Pathway combines empathy, resilience, and transformation into a comprehensive professional development experience. Offered as a 6- or 12-hour CEU series, this pathway provides reflective learning, applied coaching tools, and system-level transformation strategies for sustainable practice.
13. E.R.T.™ in Action: Integrating All Three for Sustainable Practice
14. This capstone course brings empathy, resilience, and transformation together in one cohesive model for social work excellence, professional growth, and measurable human impact.

Request a Training or Speaking Engagement

To request a keynote, CE training, certification pathway, or organizational engagement, please visit The ERT Institute at www.ertinstitute.org or through Buckingham Consulting Group, LLC at info@buckinghamcgroup.com

ASWB – ACE (Approved Continuing Education) Provider

Empathy, Resilience and Transformation (ERT) Institute, LLC, #1981, is approved as an ACE provider to offer social work continuing education by the Association of Social Work Boards (ASWB) Approved Continuing Education (ACE) program. Regulatory boards are the final authority on courses accepted for continuing education credit. ACE provider approval period: 03/31/2026 – 03/31/2029

www.ingramcontent.com/pod-product-compliance
Lightning Source LLC
LaVergne TN
LVHW090527110826
845146LV00003B/1005

* 9 7 9 8 9 9 5 3 2 7 2 0 2 *